MATH

FOR
THE GIFTED STUDENT

Challenging Activities for the Advanced Learner

Written by **Christy Yaros**

Illustrated by **Ed Shems**

GRADE **4**

Cover illustration by Steve Cox
Cover design by Gladys Lai, Loira Walsh
Interior design by Loira Walsh
Edited by Eliza Berkowitz

Flash Kids
A Division of Barnes & Noble
122 Fifth Avenue
New York, NY 10011

ISBN: 978-1-4114-2641-2

Please submit all inquiries to FlashKids@bn.com

Printed and bound in China

1 3 5 7 9 10 8 6 4 2

If you find that your child is unchallenged

by traditional workbooks and math practice drills, this workbook will provide the stimulation your student has been looking for. This workbook contains much more than typical fourth-grade drill pages and questions; it does not rely on the assumption that a gifted fourth grader simply requires fifth-grade work. The logic-based activities cover the national math standards for fourth grade while also providing kids with a chance to grow and challenge themselves beyond the work they do in the regular classroom. This workbook covers the curriculum areas of number sense, algebra, patterns, mathematical reasoning, logical thinking, measurement, geometry, graphing, probability, and statistics.

Encourage your student to use models or scrap paper to work out problems or to help him or her work through more difficult activities. Allow your student to skip around and do activities that interest him or her. The activities in the book encourage independent thinking and stimulate creativity. Your student can check his or her answers by using the answer key at the end of the book.

By utilizing this workbook series, you are providing your gifted learner an opportunity to experience scholastic achievement at an advanced level, thereby fostering confidence and an increased desire to learn.

Color the Map

Color the map using four different colors.
States that touch cannot be the same color.

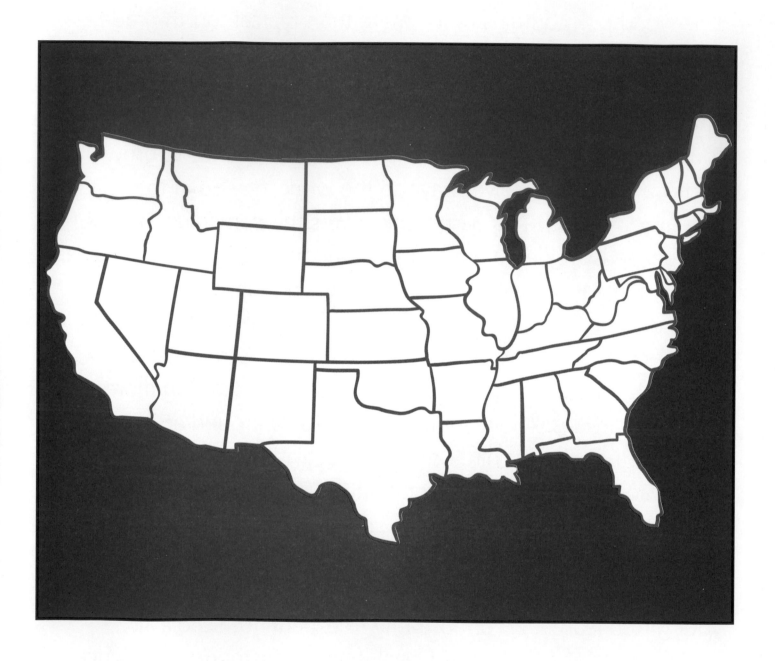

Book Comparison

Use the graphs to answer the questions below.
Then write which graph supports your answer for each.

A
Type of Books Owned

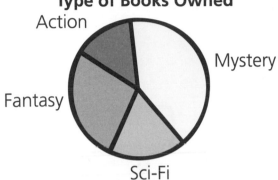

B
Favorite Type of Book for Females

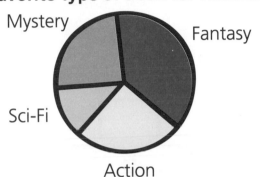

C
Favorite Type of Book for Males

D
Number of Books Sold

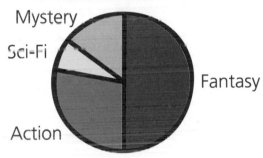

1. Which type of book do males prefer the most?

_____ _____

2. There are about half as many sci-fi books sold as which type of book?

_____ _____

3. Which type of book do the most people own?

_____ _____

4. Which is the least favorite type of book for females?

_____ _____

5. What is the second best-selling type of book?

_____ _____

6. There are about as many fantasy books owned as which two types combined?

_____ _____

Addition Pyramids

To complete each pyramid, fill the bottom row of the pyramid with the numbers given. Add two adjacent numbers and put their sum in the box above them. Continue adding until you reach the top of the pyramid.

1. 137, 345, 510, 218

2. 491, 275, 711, 364

3. 833, 352, 196, 407

4. 284, 560, 385, 609, 115

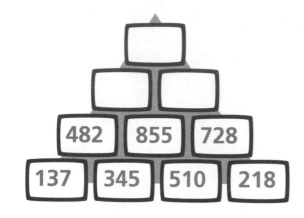

Decimal Points

Each letter in the words below is worth a certain amount of points, as shown in the table. Add up the letters to find out how many points each word is worth.

A = 2.6	H = 0.19	O = 1.2	V = 0.05
B = 0.25	I = 1.8	P = 0.11	W = 0.4
C = 2.4	J = 0.17	Q = 1.0	X = 0.03
D = 0.23	K = 1.6	R = 0.09	Y = 0.2
E = 2.2	L = 0.15	S = 0.8	Z = 0.01
F = 0.21	M = 1.4	T = 0.07	
G = 2.0	N = 0.13	U = 0.6	

1. buzzard _____

2. diamond _____

3. pineapple _____

4. octopus _____

5. telescope _____

6. represent _____

7. highway _____

8. appetite _____

9. consequence _____

10. Now find out how many your name is worth!

_____

Hexagon Math

Fill in each of the small hexagons with numbers from 1 to 9.
The six numbers around each large hexagon should add up to 35.
Numbers can be used more than once around each hexagon.

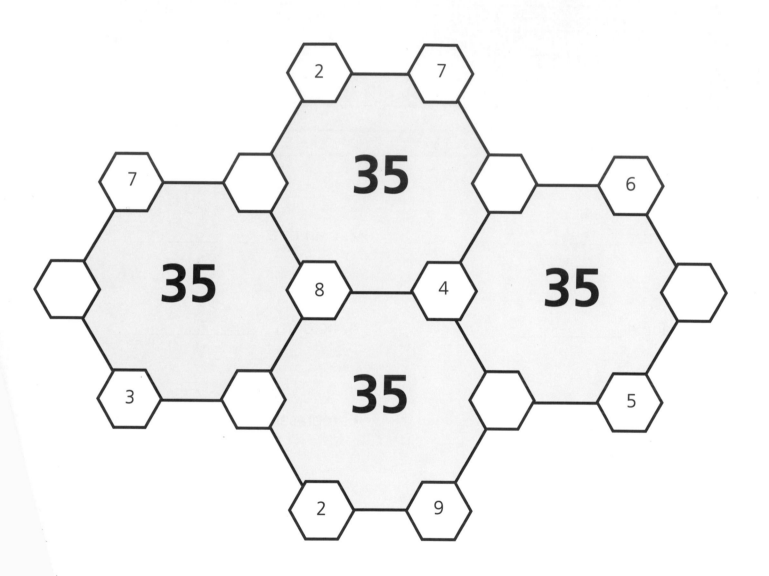

Mystery Number

Use the clues to find the mystery number. Each clue will help you eliminate one or more numbers in the chart. Place an **X** on each number you eliminate. The number that is left is the mystery number.

Clues:
- The number is odd.
- The number is divisible by 7.
- The number is less than 70.
- The number's digits added together equal more than 7.
- The number's ones digit is larger than its tens digit.
- The number is not divisible by 5.

25	50	91	54	27
18	21	42	79	10
81	36	11	60	35
26	49	58	63	14
76	47	90	32	39

What is the mystery number? _____

Corner Codes

Use the decoder below to help figure out the answer to the riddle. Notice that each letter is in its own unique shape. Each letter can be represented by drawing the shape it is in, including the dot, if there is one.

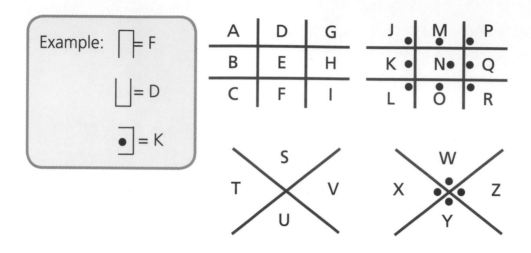

What did one math book say to the other math book?

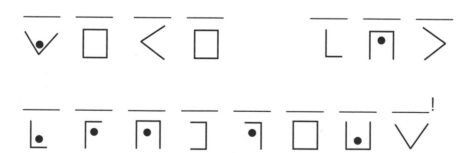

Pictographs

Use the key below to fill in any missing information or draw your own picture.

Part of School	Stands For	Example
Number of flags	Age of school (1 flag = 5 years)	15 years old
Clock	Clock = Private school or No clock = Public school	Private school
Number of windows	Number of students (1 window = 50 students)	150 students

1. Age of school: _____
   Public or private school: _____
   Number of students in school: _____

2. Age of school: _____
   Public or private school: _____
   Number of students in school: _____

3. Age of school: 20 years _____
   Public or private school: Private
   Number of students in school: 250

4. Age of school: 15 years _____
   Public or private school: Public
   Number of students in school: 300

Organizing Data

Pietra took a poll at school of her classmates' favorite animals. Look at the responses she wrote down, then answer the questions below.

Dog	Cat	Dog	Dog	Bird	Snake
Cat	Horse	Bird	Snake	Frog	Horse
Cat	Snake	Bird	Bird	Dog	Frog
Snake	Cat	Cat	Dog	Dog	Dog
Snake	Horse	Bird	Bird	Frog	Cat
Dog	Horse	Snake	Cat	Bird	Frog
Cat	Dog	Snake	Dog	Horse	Bird

1. Fill in this tally chart using Pietra's data.

Favorite Animals		
Animal	Tally	Number
Dog		
Cat		
Horse		
Frog		
Bird		
Snake		

2. How many classmates were surveyed in all? _____

3. Which animal got the most votes? _____

4. Which animal got the least votes? _____

5. Write a fraction for each animal to show how many votes it got.

Dog _____ Cat _____ Horse _____ Frog _____ Bird _____ Snake _____

6. Make a pictograph of the data. Choose a symbol that stands for 2 students.

Favorite Animals	
Dog	
Cat	
Horse	
Frog	
Bird	
Snake	

Each _____ stands for 2 students.

7. Make a bar graph using Pietra's data. Use a scale of 2.

Favorite Animals

Number of Students

| Dog | Cat | Horse | Frog | Bird | Snake |

8. Make a pie chart using the data.

Favorite Animals

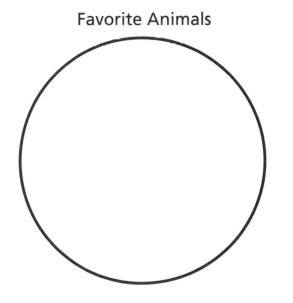

Calendar Magic

Follow the directions below for a fun calendar trick that you can try with your friends!

Have a friend choose any 4 days from the calendar that form a square. Tell him or her to add up the numbers and tell you the sum. Now you can tell your friend which 4 days he or she chose! All you have to do is follow the directions:

1. Divide the sum he or she gives you by 4.
2. Now subtract 4. That's the first day.
3. Add 1 to the first day for the second day.
4. Add 7 to the first day for the third day.
5. Add 8 to the first day for the fourth day.

Practice a few before you try it on your friends. Now write which block of 4 days on the calendar goes with these sums.

1. 108 _____

2. 72 _____

3. 20 _____

4. 56 _____

5. 92 _____

6. 40 _____

More Calendar Magic

Here's another calendar trick that you can try on your friends.

This time have a friend choose any 3 days that form an L, like 1, 8, and 9. Tell him or her to add up the numbers and tell you the sum. Now you can tell your friend which 3 days he or she chose! All you have to do is follow the directions:

1. Divide the sum he or she gives you by 3.
2. Subtract 5 from Step 1 to get the first number.
3. Add 7 to that number to get the second number.
4. Add 1 to that number to get the third number.

Practice a few before you try it on your friends. Now write which 3 days in the shape of an L on the calendar go with these sums.

1. 36 _____

2. 81 _____

3. 75 _____

4. 45 _____

5. 24 _____

6. 63 _____

Tasha and Leanne have a secret code they use to send messages.
Use the code to figure out what message Tasha sent Leanne.

ABC	DEF	GHI
< - >	< - >	< - >
JKL	MNO	PQR
< - >	< - >	< - >
STU	VWX	YZ
< - >	< - >	< -

Hint: 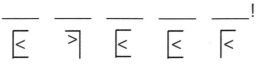 = A B C

Message:

Egyptian Numbers

This is the number system that the ancient Egyptians used.

$\mid$ = 1		= 10		= 100		= 1,000		= 10,000	

= 100,000   = 1,000,000

Write these numbers using Egyptian numerals.

1. 1,254 _____

2. 24,761 _____

3. 633,507 _____

4. 1,354,680 _____

Now write these Egyptian numerals in standard numerals.

5. 𓏤𓏤𓏤𓏤𓏤 𓆼𓆼𓆼 𓎆𓎆𓎆𓏤𓏤𓏤𓏤𓏤𓏤 _____

6. _____

_____

7. _____

8. _____

Factor Trees

Fill in the missing numbers to complete the factor trees.

1.

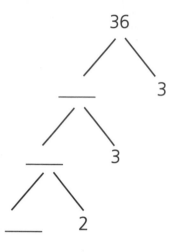

36
3
___
3
___
2
___

2.

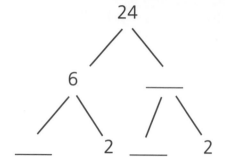

24
6
___
___   2   ___   2

3.

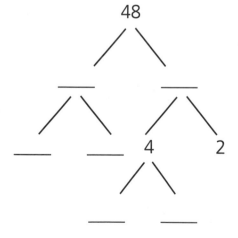

48
___   ___
___   ___   4   2
___   ___

4. Draw four different factor trees for 60.

Graph a Riddle

Plot the points on the graph below and label them with their letter.

A (2, 4)	B (6, 7)	C (14, 4)	D (15, 10)	E (5, 10)
F (10, 10)	G (18, 4)	H (9, 7)	I (2, 10)	J (6, 4)
K (18, 10)	L (5, 4)	M (9, 4)	N (12, 4)	O (6, 10)
P (10, 4)	Q (9, 10)	R (14, 10)	S (15, 4)	T (12, 10)

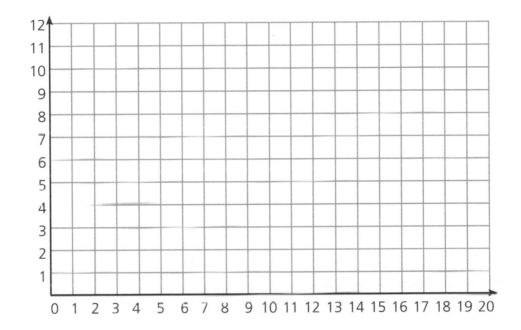

Now draw these line segments on the graph and read the answer to the riddle below.

ET	AT
AL	EL
JO	MQ
FR	NT
CP	DK
DS	GS
GK	BH

What state is round on the ends and high in the middle? _____

Nancy's Number

Nancy is thinking of a number from 1 to 100. Read the clues to find out what number she is thinking of. Each clue will help you eliminate one or more numbers in the chart. Place an **X** on each number you eliminate. The number that is left is Nancy's number.

Clues:

- Nancy's number has two digits.
- Nancy's number is not a multiple of 7.
- Nancy's number is a multiple of 4.
- The digits in Nancy's number add up to 7.
- The ones digit of Nancy's number is less than the tens digit.

1	2	3	4	5	6	7	8	9	10
11	12	13	14	15	16	17	18	19	20
21	22	23	24	25	26	27	28	29	30
31	32	33	34	35	36	37	38	39	40
41	42	43	44	45	46	47	48	49	50
51	52	53	54	55	56	57	58	59	60
61	62	63	64	65	66	67	68	69	70
71	72	73	74	75	76	77	78	79	80
81	82	83	84	85	86	87	88	89	90
91	92	93	94	95	96	97	98	99	100

What number is Nancy thinking of? _____

Cookie Sales

The fourth-grade class at Lakeville Elementary sold cookies to raise money for a new playground. Fill in the chart by drawing cookies to represent how many boxes of cookies were sold by each class. One cookie should represent 8 boxes sold.

Class	Boxes Sold	Class	Boxes Sold
Room 401	64	Room 401	
Room 402	44	Room 402	
Room 403	24	Room 403	
Room 404	34	Room 404	
Room 405	56	Room 405	
Room 406	48	Room 406	

Each represents 8 boxes.

1. Which class did you draw 6 cookies for? _____

2. Which class did you draw 4.25 cookies for? _____

3. If the boxes sold for Room 401 were represented by 4 cookies, then how much would each cookie represent? _____

4. How many cookies would you draw to represent the total amount of boxes sold for all the classes in the fourth grade? _____

Angela's Awesome Angles

Angela drew the following picture of a boat. Use the drawing to help Angela identify the types of angles shown.

Find 4 obtuse angles and mark them with an **O**.
Find 9 acute angles and mark them with an **A**.
Find 8 right angles and mark them with an **R**.

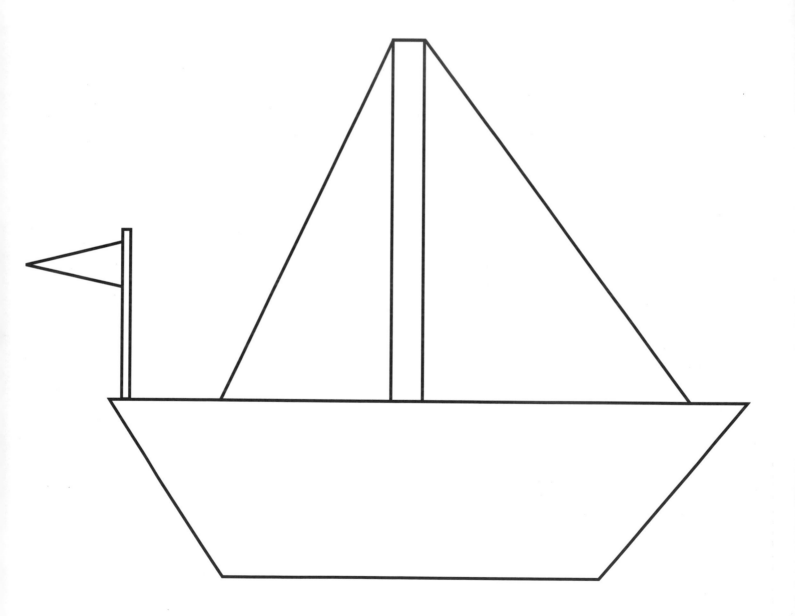

Adios, Addition!
Sayonara, Subtraction!

Add **+** and **−** signs to make each number sentence true.

1. 6 ☐ 3 ☐ 2 = 5

2. 80 ☐ 37 ☐ 51 = 66

3. 65 ☐ 3 ☐ 4 = 58

4. 77 ☐ 4 ☐ 3 = 78

5. 60 ☐ 6 ☐ 38 ☐ 9 = 95

6. 76 ☐ 19 ☐ 46 ☐ 1 = 142

7. 97 ☐ 11 ☐ 49 ☐ 19 − 116

8. 8 ☐ 37 ☐ 33 = 4

Circle Circus

Write the sum of the numbers in the circles where they overlap.
The first one has been done for you.

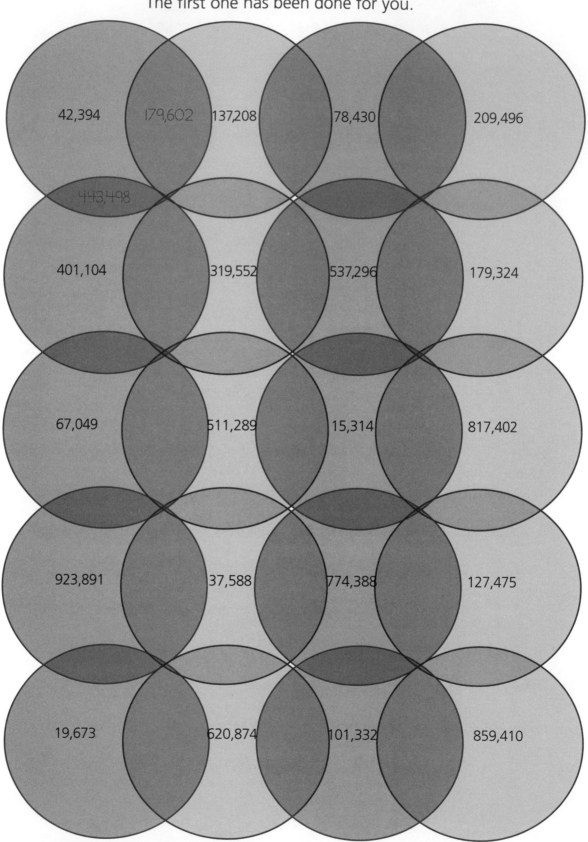

42,394 179,602 137,208 78,430 209,496

443,498

401,104 319,552 537,296 179,324

67,049 511,289 15,314 817,402

923,891 37,588 774,388 127,475

19,673 620,874 101,332 859,410

Polygonal Angles

If you divide a polygon into triangles, you can find the sum of the interior angles. To divide a polygon into triangles, choose one corner and draw as many diagonals as you can from that corner to other corners. Then count up the triangles. Multiply that number by 180°.

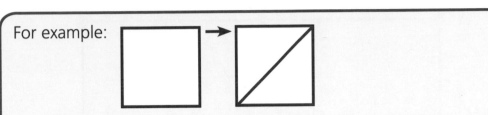

For example:

By drawing lines from one corner, a square can be divided into 2 triangles. A triangle has 180°, so multiply 180 by 2 to get 360°.

Find the sum of the interior angles for each shape below.

1.

_____

2.

_____

3.

_____

4.

_____

5.

_____

6.

_____

Polygon Parts

Use the figure below to answer the questions.

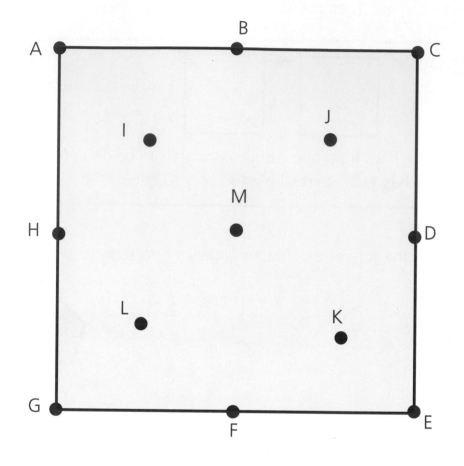

1. Connect point *A* to point *E*. What shape is formed by *ACE*? _____

What fraction of the total square is it? _____

2. Connect point *B* to point *F*. What fraction of the square is *MEF*?

_____

3. Connect point *B* to point *H*. What fraction of the square is *AIH*?

_____

4. Connect point *B* to point *D*, point *D* to point *F*, and point *F* to point *H*. What shape is formed by *BDFH*? _____

What fraction of the square is it? _____

5. What fraction of the square is *HBF*? _____

6. Connect point *C* to point *G* and point *H* to point *D*. How many triangles are in the figure? _____ How many squares?

_____

7. What kind of angle is ∠*BMK*? _____

8. What kind of angle is ∠*DMK*? _____

9. What kind of angle is ∠*IML*? _____

10. Are lines *EF* and *MD* parallel or perpendicular? _____

11. Are lines *FG* and *BM* parallel or perpendicular? _____

12. Name a triangle that is congruent to *AIH*. _____

For an extra challenge, find a parallelogram and a trapezoid.

Polygon Areas

Find the area of each figure.

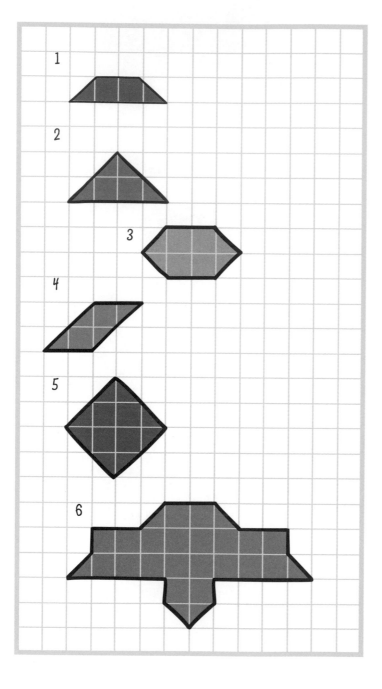

1. _____

2. _____

3. _____

4. _____

5. _____

6. _____

Time to Spare

Use the information in the box below to complete each problem.

1 minute = 60 seconds
1 hour = 60 minutes
1 day = 24 hours
1 week = 7 days
1 year = 365 days
1 year = 12 months

1. 31 days = _____ weeks ___ days

2. 46 months = _____ years _____ months

3. 57 hours = _____ days _____ hours

4. 182 seconds = _____ minutes _____ seconds

5. 3 years 6 months = _____ months

6. 5 hours 23 minutes = _____ minutes

7. 8 weeks 4 days = _____ days

8. 3 days 2 hours = _____ hours

Quadrilateral Commotion

Alex is in trouble! Her puppy knocked over all the signs in her uncle's shop, Cute Quadrilaterals, and ruined them. Can you help her put the signs back on the quadrilaterals before the store opens?

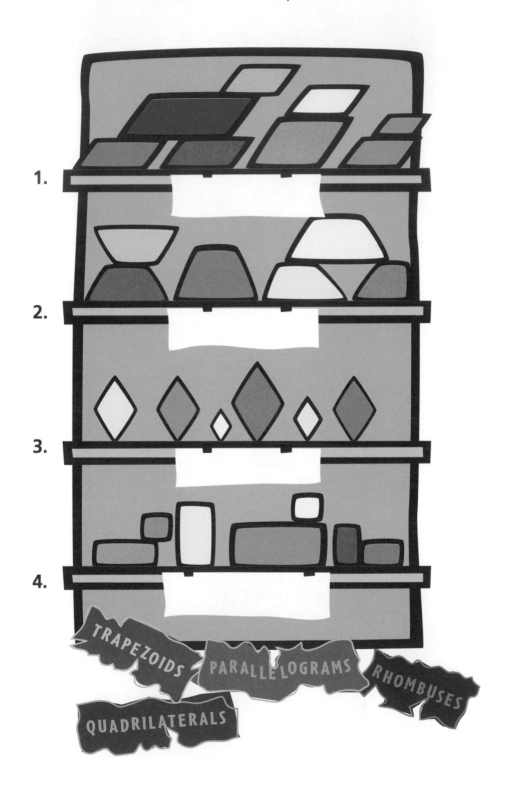

Roman Numerals

The Romans used letters to write their numbers. Use the information in the box to figure out what numbers are represented by the Roman numerals below. If a smaller number is before a larger one, subtract them to get the value of the number.

```
I = 1          C = 100
V = 5          D = 500
X = 10         M = 1,000
L = 50

Remember these shortcuts:
III = 1 + 1 + 1 = 3      XL = 50 − 10 = 40
IV = 5 − 1 = 4           CD = 500 − 100 = 400
VI = 5 + 1 = 6           CM = 1,000 − 100 = 900
IX = 10 − 1 = 9          MC = 1,000 + 100 = 1,100
```

1. XVII _____

2. XXXIV _____

3. LXI _____

4. MXCIV _____

5. MDCCXLV _____

Now write the Roman numerals that would represent each number below.

6. 38 _____

7. 364 _____

8. 3,472 _____

9. 2,987 _____

10. 1,293 _____

Repeating Decimal Patterns

When the numbers 9, 99, or 999 are the denominator of a fraction, you get a special repeating decimal. There is a pattern to convert these fractions to decimals without dividing. Look at the pattern in the box, then use it to convert the fractions below to decimals.

$$\frac{1}{9} = 0.111\ldots \qquad \frac{1}{99} = 0.010101\ldots \qquad \frac{1}{999} = 0.001001001\ldots$$

$$\frac{12}{99} = 0.121212\ldots \qquad \frac{12}{999} = 0.012012012\ldots$$

$$\frac{123}{999} = 0.123123123\ldots$$

1. $\frac{34}{99} = $ _____

2. $\frac{4}{9} = $ _____

3. $\frac{867}{999} = $ _____

4. $\frac{9}{999} = $ _____

5. $\frac{78}{99} = $ _____

6. $\frac{2}{9} = $ _____

7. $\frac{5}{99} = $ _____

8. $\frac{998}{999} = $ _____

9. $\frac{62}{999} = $ _____

10. $\frac{70}{999} = $ _____

Family Reunion

Jenna wants to plan a family reunion for her great-grandmother's 85th birthday. Jenna lives in Dallas, while the rest of her family lives all over the country. Use the time-zone map to answer the questions below.

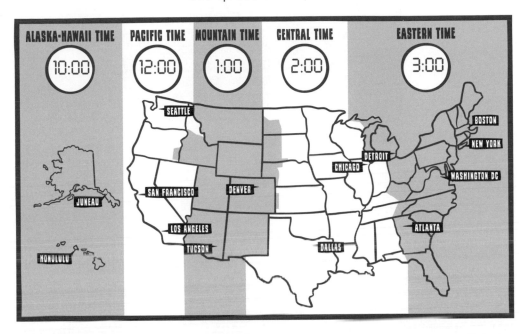

1. If it is 9:00 AM in Jenna's house, what time is it in these other cities?

Atlanta	Boston	Chicago	Dallas	Denver	Detroit	Honolulu

Juneau	Los Angeles	New York	San Francisco	Seattle	Tucson	Washington, D.C.

2. What would be the earliest Jenna can call her family in Juneau if she doesn't want to disturb anyone before 9:00 AM? _____

3. What would be the latest Jenna can call her family in New York City if she doesn't want it to bother anyone after 8:00 PM? _____

4. What time is it in your city when it is 4:00 PM for Jenna? _____

Taj's Town

Use the coordinate grid below to plot and label the places in Taj's town.
Then answer the questions that follow.

Home	(2, 7)
School	(7, 7)
Park	(0, 3)
Store	(0, 6)
Min's House	(4, 3)
Library	(9, 3)

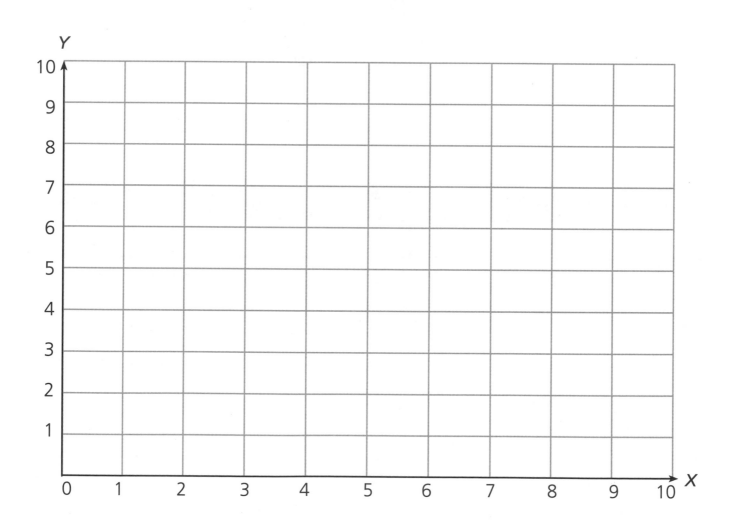

1. If Taj travels from home to school to the library to the park and back home, what figure is made?

_____

2. If Taj travels from home to Min's house to the library to school and back home, what figure is made?

_____

3. If Taj travels from home to Min's house to the park and back home, what figure is made? _____

4. How many units are between the store and the park?

_____

5. How many units are between Taj's house and the school?

_____

6. Name three other routes that Taj can travel to make a triangle.

_____

_____

_____

7. Is the road that Taj's home and school are on parallel or perpendicular to the road that the park and the library are on? _____

8. Is the road that the store and park are on parallel or perpendicular to the road that Min's house and the library are on? _____

9. What kind of angle does the route of school to home to the store make?

_____

10. What kind of angle does the route of school to Min's house to the library make? _____

11. What kind of angle does the route of the store to the park to Min's house make? _____

12. If Taj traveled in a rectangle from the store to the park to Min's house to the museum, where must the museum be? _____

Divisibility by 3

Here's a trick for checking if a number can be divided by 3 with no remainder.

> 1. Add the digits of the given number. Repeat until you have a one-digit number.
> 2. If the answer is 3, 6, or 9, then the given number is evenly divisible by 3.
>
> For example: $451{,}347{,}964 \longrightarrow 4 + 5 + 1 + 3 + 4 + 7 + 9 + 6 + 4 = 43$
> $\qquad\qquad\qquad 4 + 3 = 7$
> Seven is not 3, 6, or 9. So, 451,347,964 is not evenly divisible by 3.

Use the trick to quickly see if each number below can be divided by 3 with no remainder.
Write *yes* or *no*.

1. 78,541,359 _____

2. 46,597,133 _____

3. 54,649,463 _____

4. 74,313,492 _____

5. 459,743,169 _____

6. 794,131,546 _____

7. 124,579,315 _____

8. 214,536,989 _____

Divisibility by 4

Here's a trick for checking if a number can be divided by 4 with no remainder.

> If the last two digits are evenly divisible by 4, then the entire number is evenly divisible by 4.
>
> For example: 54,123,676 $\longrightarrow$ $\dfrac{76}{4} = 19$
>
> So, 54,123,676 is evenly divisible by 4.

Use the trick to quickly see if each number below can be divided by 4 with no remainder. Write *yes* or *no*.

1. 51,246,988　　　　　_____

2. 32,659,876　　　　　_____

3. 36,529,685　　　　　_____

4. 23,659,874　　　　　_____

5. 745,329,848　　　　_____

6. 123,456,859　　　　_____

7. 652,347,812　　　　_____

8. 316,549,754　　　　_____

Divisibility by 6

Here's a trick for checking if a number can be divided by 6 with no remainder.

> 1. The number must be even.
> 2. If the sum of the digits is 3, 6, or 9, then the entire number is divisible by 6.
>
> For example: 53,269,854
> 1. It is even.
> 2. 53,269,854 ⟶ 5 + 3 + 2 + 6 + 9 + 8 + 5 + 4 = 42
>   4 + 2 = 6.
> So, 53,269,854 is evenly divisible by 6.

Use the trick to quickly see if each number below can be divided by 6 with no remainder.
Write *yes* or *no*.

1. 65,265,987 _____

2. 23,659,874 _____

3. 69,856,326 _____

4. 85,316,958 _____

5. 3,268,986,498 _____

6. 4,695,385,637 _____

7. 8,965,352,368 _____

8. 5,698,563,524 _____

Divisibility by 8

Here's a trick for checking if a number can be divided by 8 with no remainder.

If the last three digits of the number are divisible by 8, then the number is divisible by 8.

Here's a trick for checking if the last three digits are evenly divisible by 8:
If the first digit is even and the last two digits are divisible by 8, then the number is divisible by 8.
If the first digit is odd and the last two digits minus 4 are divisible by 8, then the number is divisible by 8.

For example: 5,594,184
1. Look at the last three digits: 184.
2. The first digit is odd, so subtract 4 from the last two digits: 84 – 4 = 80.
3. The result is evenly divisible by 8, so the entire number is divisible by 8.

Use the trick to quickly see if each number below can be divided by 8 with no remainder.
Write *yes* or *no*.

1. 483,593,284 _____

2. 897,106,792 _____

3. 619,392,996 _____

4. 109,852,267 _____

5. 487,094,064 _____

6. 359,617,512 _____

7. 752,903,872 _____

8. 583,410,762 _____

Divisibility by 9

Here's a trick for checking if a number can be divided by 9 with no remainder.

> If the sum of the digits is 9 or a number easily recognizable as a multiple of 9, then the number is divisible by 9.
>
> For example: $3,659,745,312 \longrightarrow 3 + 6 + 5 + 9 + 7 + 4 + 5 + 3 + 1 + 2 = 45$
> $4 + 5 = 9$
> So, 3,659,745,312 is evenly divisible by 9.

Use the trick to quickly see if each number below can be divided by 9 with no remainder.
Write *yes* or *no*.

1. 429,875,132 _____

2. 894,234,564 _____

3. 632,659,875 _____

4. 986,417,568 _____

5. 359,857,854 _____

6. 265,369,846 _____

7. 589,642,235 _____

8. 965,463,669 _____

Code Club

The Code Club uses secret codes to send messages to each other. Each week a different member makes up the code to be used until the next meeting. This week it's Sam's turn. Fill in the rest of his code using the pattern he started.

A	1
B	3
C	7
D	9
E	13
F	
G	
H	
I	
J	
K	
L	
M	
N	
O	
P	
Q	
R	
S	
T	
U	
V	
W	
X	
Y	
Z	

Sam sent this message to Matt.
Can you use this code to decipher it?

3-13-9

9-43   73-43-61   67-1-39-57

____ __   ____ ____ __   ____ ____ ____ __

57-43   7-43-37-13   43-63-13-51

____ __   __ __ __ __   ____ ____ ____ ____

1-15-57-13-51   55-7-21-43-43-33

____ __ __ __ __   ____ __ __ __ __ __ ?

Now write your own message using Sam's code:

Division with Remainders

Solve the problems below.

1. Kelly brings 32 apples to school for her class. There are 15 kids in her class. How many apples will she have left over if everyone gets the same amount?

   _____

2. Eli has 43 homework problems. If he does 20 problems every hour, then how many problems will he have left to do the last hour?

   _____

3. Tasha is packing her books in boxes to move to a new place. She has 54 books and each box can hold 10 books. How many books will be in the last box? _____

4. A class of 37 needs to split into 5 even groups of people. How many people will be left over? _____

5. A bag of pretzels has 72 pretzels in it. If someone eats 13 pretzels every day, then how many pretzels are left on the last day? _____

6. A water bucket has 103 cups of water in it. Each day 9 cups of water leak out of it. How many cups leak out on the last day? _____

Geometric Sequences

Geometric sequences are number patterns in which each number is found by multiplying or dividing by a certain number. Find the next number in these patterns and describe the pattern.

1. 1; 8; 64; 512;

_____

Pattern: _____

2. 16,807; 2,401; 343; 49;

_____

Pattern: _____

3. 121; 1,331; 14,641; 161,051;

_____

Pattern: _____

4. 216; 1,296; 7,776; 46,656;

_____

Pattern: _____

5. 640; 320; 160; 80;

_____

Pattern: _____

6. 25; 125; 625; 3,125;

_____

Pattern: _____

7. 1,000,000; 100,000; 10,000; 1,000;

_____

Pattern: _____

8. 256; 1,024; 4,096; 16,384;

_____

Pattern: _____

9. 169; 2,197; 28,561; 371,293;

_____

Pattern: _____

10. 531,441; 59,049; 6,561; 729;

_____

Pattern: _____

Hundredths

Write each decimal as a fraction. Then use the grids below to shade the amount shown. Be creative in the patterns you use!

1. $0.28 = \dfrac{\square}{\square}$

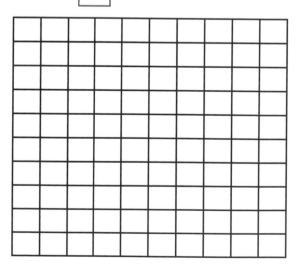

2. $0.74 = \dfrac{\square}{\square}$

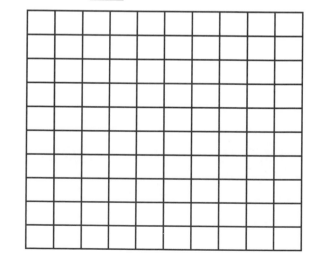

3. $0.62 = \dfrac{\square}{\square}$

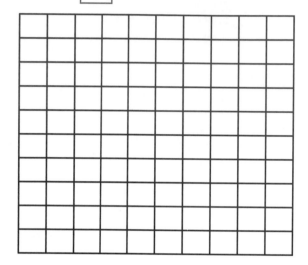

4. $0.56 = \dfrac{\square}{\square}$

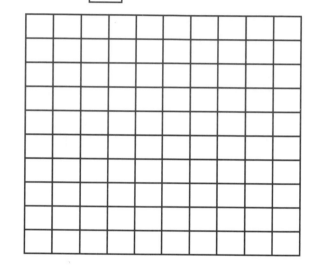

One Step at a Time

Solve the multistep problems below.

1. Gabrielle has a collection of stuffed animals. She has 7 dogs in her collection. She has 4 more cats than she has dogs and she has 2 more bears than she has cats. How many stuffed animals does Gabrielle have? _____

2. Lenny's dad took him out for lunch. They had 2 sandwiches and 2 sodas. Each sandwich cost $2.55 and each soda cost $1.05. Tax was $1.40. How much change should Lenny's dad get back from a 10-dollar bill?

   _____

3. Penny bought 3 hair clips for $0.70 each and 2 bracelets for $1.20 each. The next day Penny bought 4 rings for $1.25 each and 1 hat for $2.25. How much more money did Penny spend on the second day than on the first?

   _____

4. Albert collects baseball cards. He had 23 cards in his collection. He got 6 for his birthday and his brother gave him 4. Albert then gave his friend 11 of his cards. How many baseball cards does Albert have left? _____

5. Vanessa is 8 years old. If you add 4 to her age and triple it, then you get the age of her older sister. How old is Vanessa's sister? _____

6. Michael wants to buy a game that costs $10.00, a shirt that costs $8.00, and an action figure that costs $3.00. Michael has $15.00. How much more money does Michael need to buy all of the items he wants? _____

Pentapuzzle

Going clockwise, fill in the circles below to make each pentagon correct. A number is added to the previous circle to get the next answer. The same number is added to each circle within the same pentagon.

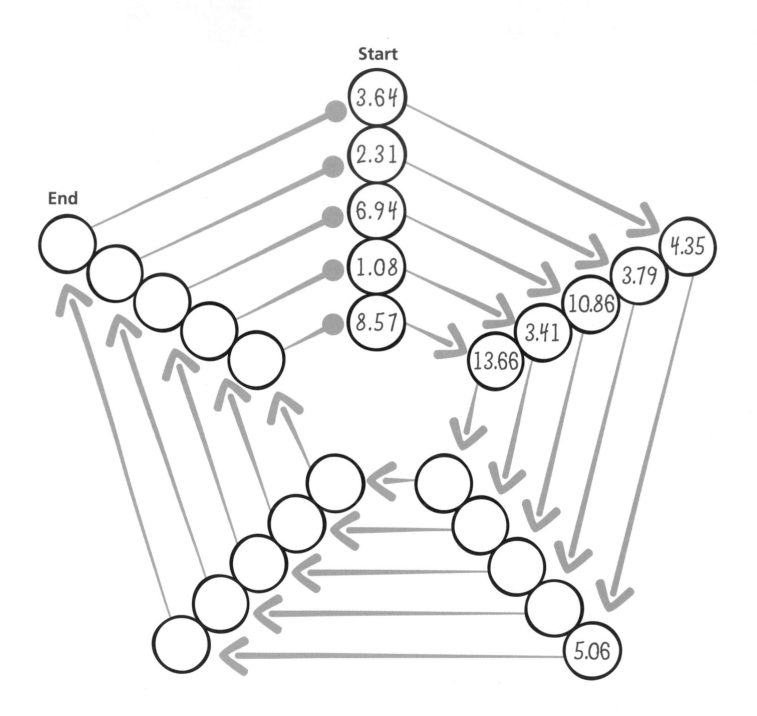

Not So Simple

The mixed numbers below are not in simplest form. Shade the circles to show each mixed number and then write the mixed number in simplest form.

1. $1\frac{5}{2}$ $1\frac{5}{2} =$ _____

2. $2\frac{5}{3}$ $2\frac{5}{3} =$ _____

3. $3\frac{6}{4}$ $3\frac{6}{4} =$ _____

4. $3\frac{13}{5}$ $3\frac{13}{5} =$ _____

5. $4\frac{11}{6}$ $4\frac{11}{6} =$ _____

6. $2\frac{27}{8}$ $2\frac{27}{8} =$ _____

7. $3\frac{30}{10}$ $3\frac{30}{10} =$ _____

8. $2\frac{40}{12}$ $2\frac{40}{12} =$ _____

A Perfect Ten!

Judges at the Brooklyn Academy's gymnastics meet give each gymnast a score from 0 to 10. Ten is a perfect score. The average of all the judges' scores determines the final score. Find the average of each gymnast's score to the nearest hundredth.

1. | Kelly | 7.4 | 8.1 | 7.6 | 8.5 |

_____

2. | Juan | 8.3 | 6.9 | 7.0 | 8.1 |

_____

3. | Zoe | 9.1 | 8.2 | 7.9 | 8.0 |

_____

4. | Sven | 7.9 | 9.3 | 8.5 | 8.4 |

_____

5. | Etienne | 8.8 | 8.9 | 8.8 | 8.1 |

_____

6. | Carlos | 7.8 | 8.2 | 9.0 | 7.5 |

_____

Now put the gymnasts' averages in order from greatest to least to see who won.

Place	Gymnast
Gold	
Silver	
Bronze	
4th	
5th	
6th	

Fibonacci Sequences

In 1202, a man named Fibonacci introduced a sequence of numbers we now call Fibonacci numbers. The sequence follows a special pattern. It starts with 0 and 1, and then each number following is the sum of the two before it. Look at the example in the box, then complete the pattern below.

$$0, 1, 1, 2, 3, 5, 8,\dots$$

0,	1,	1,	2,	3,	5,	8,	___	___	___
___	___	___	___	___	___	___	___	___	___
___	___	___	___	___	___	___	___	___	___

Look at the numbers you filled in. Do you see any other patterns?

_____

_____

Marty's Map

Use the map to help Marty get where he needs to go.

1. Marty is trying to get to his friend's house at the corner of Oak Ave. and Winter St. He is currently at the corner of Spring St. and Maple Ave. He hears that Oak St. is closed from Winter St. to Spring St. Which roads can he take to avoid the closed road and travel the shortest distance? _____

2. If Marty decides that he wants to drive parallel to the river for as long as possible to get to his friend's house while still traveling the shortest distance, then which roads should he take? _____

3. After Marty visits his friend, he wants to go see the new store he heard about. He knows it is on a street parallel to Fall St., but he can't remember which one. On which streets could the store be located? _____

4. Marty decides to go to the store when he is at the corner of Maple Ave. and Winter St. On the way to the store, he has to turn around because a tree has fallen across Winter St between Birch Ave. and Maple Ave. Which perpendicular road should he take to get around the tree in the easiest possible way? _____

5. Marty's dad tells him that the new store is on the corner of Spring St. and the westernmost road that is perpendicular to it. Where is the store located?

_____

Remainder Riddle

Solve the problems below. Use the letter for each remainder to complete the riddle at the bottom of the page.

1. R = $6\overline{)472}$

2. O = $7\overline{)359}$

3. N = $3\overline{)91}$

4. E = $4\overline{)675}$

5. A = $8\overline{)999}$

6. Y = $9\overline{)719}$

7. M = $5\overline{)635}$

8. U = $6\overline{)893}$

What belongs to you, but others use more than you?

___ ___ ___ ___   ___ ___ ___ ___ !
 8   2   5   4   1   7   0   3

Remainders as Fractions

When you have a remainder left over after you divide, it can be written as a fraction. To do this just take the remainder that you get and put it over the number you were dividing by. See the example inside the box, then write the answers to the division problems below using fractions for remainders.

Example: $20 \div 6 = 3\ R2$ or $3\,\dfrac{2}{6}$

1. $6\overline{)45}$ = _____

2. $7\overline{)325}$ = _____

3. $4\overline{)73}$ = _____

4. $8\overline{)525}$ = _____

5. $9\overline{)2,593}$ = _____

6. $5\overline{)8,017}$ = _____

7. $3\overline{)67,309}$ = _____

8. $7\overline{)174,634}$ = _____

Puzzling Place Value

Follow the instructions below. Write each answer in the correct place value box on the chart to find the seven-digit number.

1,000,000s	100,000s	10,000s	1,000s	100s	10s	1s

Divide 72 by 8. Subtract 5, and write the result in the ones place.

Double the number in the ones place and add 1. Write the result in the thousands place.

Multiply 8 by 11. Subtract it from 93. Write the result in the hundred thousands place.

Divide the number in the thousands place by 3. Add it to the number in the hundred thousands place. Write the result in the hundreds place.

Halve the number in the ones place. Multiply by 3, and write the result in the millions place.

Divide 28 by the number in the ones place. Write the result in the ten thousands place.

Write the number 3 in the remaining place.

Now write the complete number in words.

_____

_____

More Puzzling Place Values

Follow the instructions below. Write each answer in the correct place value on the lines in the box to find the eight-digit number.

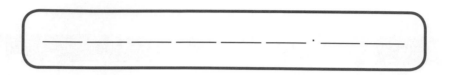

Divide 211 by itself. Write the result in the ones place.

Double the number in the ones place. Write the result in the hundreds place.

Subtract the number of hours in a day from the number of days in April. Write the result in the tenths place.

Halve the number in the tenths place. Write the result in the thousands place.

Multiply the number in the thousands place by itself. Write the result in the tens place.

Divide the number of hours in three days by the number in the tens place. Write the result in the ten thousands place.

Find the number of hours between 11:00 AM and 1:00 PM, and write the result in the hundred thousands place.

Add the number in the hundreds place, the number in the hundred thousands place, and the number in the thousands place together. Write the result in the hundredths place.

The Perez Family

Fill in the bar graph and the number line based on the information in the table. Then answer the questions below.

Age of Family Members of the Perez Family

Name	Age (in Years)
Ramon	38
Maria	37
Rafael	12
Lucinda	7
Sal	65
Anna	62

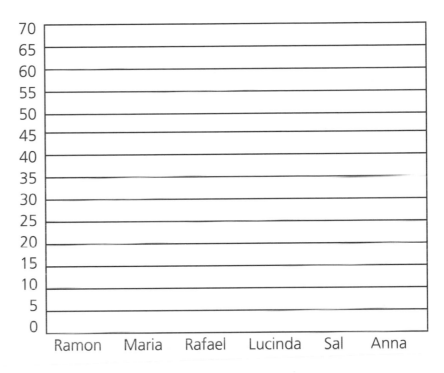

1. What is the range of ages? _____

2. What is the average age to the nearest hundredth? _____

3. What is the median age? _____

4. If cousins Bonita, 15, and Esai, 17, are included, what is the new mean age to the nearest hundredth? _____

Tallying Time

Add or subtract. Rename when necessary.

1.   2 h 20 min
   + 3 h 15 min
   _____

2.   8 h 43 min
   − 8 h 18 min
   _____

3.   6 h 9 min
   + 4 h 36 min
   _____

4.   4 h 36 min
   − 3 h 14 min
   _____

5.   7 h 12 min
   + 2 h 56 min
   _____

6.   3 h 12 min
   − 2 h 45 min
   _____

7.   6 h 13 min
   + 4 h 47 min
   _____

8.   4 h 25 min
   − 1 h 40 min
   _____

Simple Symmetry

Draw all the lines of symmetry on these shapes. Note: not all shapes may have symmetry.

1.

2.

3.

4.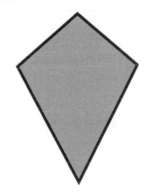

5.

6.

7.

8.

Rounding Route

Find the best route through the city by following the properly rounded addition or subtraction problems. First round the numbers to the nearest tenth or hundredth, then add or subtract. Mark the path of the problems that are rounded correctly.

$27.49 + 13.16 = 40.7$

$943.634 - 359.942 = 583.69$

$7.29 + 11.07 = 18.4$

$39.32 + 58.27 = 97.5$

$56.31 + 41.57 = 97.8$

$43,984.693 + 29,153.319 = 73,138$

$557.31 - 321.74 = 235.5$

$64,693.617 + 16,367.391 = 81,061.01$

$482.115 + 5,406.438 = 5,888.55$

$693.195 - 284.558 = 408.64$

$65.29 + 58.52 = 123.7$

$25,391.51 + 472.35 = 25,863.9$

$19.57 + 293.52 = 313$

$97.28 - 55.09 = 42.2$

$789,493.229 - 539,054.838 = 250,438.4$

$59.136 + 36.925 = 96.07$

$5,490.155 - 2,318.503 = 3,171.66$

START

END

Spin to Win!

Color the spinner to match these probabilities:

• The probability of landing on blue is $\frac{1}{3}$.

• The probability of landing on green is $\frac{1}{2}$.

• The probability of landing on red is $\frac{1}{6}$.

• The probability of landing on yellow is $\frac{0}{12}$.

Now use the spinner to answer these questions.

1. Which color do you have the greatest chance of landing on? _____

2. Which color do you have the least chance of landing on? _____

3. Which are you more likely to land on: red or yellow? _____

4. Which are you less likely to land on: green or blue? _____

Pizza Party

Today there was a pizza party. Mitch ate 0.5 of a pizza. Paula ate 0.25 of a pizza. Larry ate three eighths of a pizza. Helene ate five eighths of a pizza. Shade the pizzas below to show how much pizza each person ate. Then write each person's name in order from the least eaten to the most eaten.

Mitch

Paula

Larry

Helene

Least eaten _____ _____ _____ _____ Most eaten

Canine Club

The Canine Club of Canton is having its annual picnic. The photo below is a group picture of the people and dogs who attended. Make sure to answer the questions in fraction form.

1. How many of the people are male?

$\frac{7}{13}$ _____

2. How many of the people are wearing glasses? _____

3. How many of the animals are **not** spotted? _____

4. How many of the people have short hair? _____

5. How many of the dogs are white? _____

6. How many of the animals are golden? _____

7. How many of the children have hats? _____

8. How many of the people are **not** children? _____

9. How many of the adults have hats? _____

10. How many in the group picture are animals? _____

Checks and Balances

Congratulations! You just opened your first bank account. It is important that you keep a record of anything you deposit (put into) or withdraw (take out of) your account so that you know how much money you have. Look below for each debit or credit you need to fill in. Use the information to fill in the checking account ledger on the next page. The first two lines of your ledger have been filled in for you.

1. Deposit $347.23 to open your account.

2. Withdraw $50.75 for that new video game that came out!

3. You earned $25.50 mowing lawns to put into your account.

4. You found the perfect gift for your mother's birthday. It cost you $22.45.

5. Your little sister needs to borrow $10.20 so she can buy your mother a gift, too.

6. Your chores are done! You deposit your $5.00 allowance.

7. Your fish tank needs some supplies. They cost $32.75.

8. Your favorite band has a new CD out. You withdraw $19.99 to buy it.

9. On the way out of the store you see that DVD you have been wanting. You go back and buy it for $18.33.

10. You earn $0.90 in interest for the month.

TRANSACTIONS	DEBIT (−) (WITHDRAWAL)		CREDIT (+) (DEPOSIT)		BALANCE	
Deposit			$347	23	$347	23
Video game withdrawal	−$50	75			$296	48

What is the remaining balance of your bank account? _____

Alphabet Areas

Find the area of each of the letters below.

1.

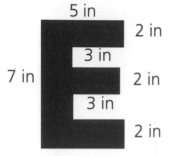

5 in
2 in
3 in
7 in
2 in
3 in
2 in

2.

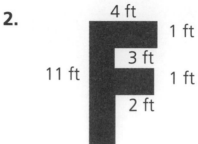

4 ft
1 ft
3 ft
11 ft
1 ft
2 ft

3.

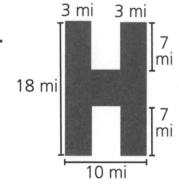

3 mi   3 mi
7 mi
18 mi
7 mi
10 mi

4.

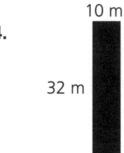

10 m
32 m

5.

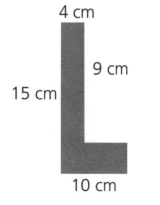

4 cm
9 cm
15 cm
10 cm

6.

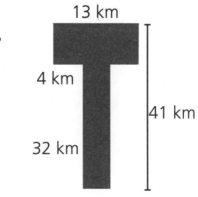

13 km
4 km
41 km
32 km

Decimal Puzzles

To complete each puzzle, write the missing numbers in the pink boxes. The sum of each row, column, and diagonal is given to you in the green boxes.

1.

			8.79

	9.25	4.63	22.20
3.93			10.59
	7.18	5.05	15.02

15.04	17.80	14.97	14.74

2.

			18.37

4.32		5.97	12.02
		6.81	21.75
3.06	7.62		13.19

12.98	18.69	15.29	16.17

3.

			18.52

		2.19	11.32
4.63			15.10
8.35	1.08		13.18

16.47	14.70	8.43	15.22

4.

			15.89

	2.49		15.36
			12.59
1.99		4.73	12.24

9.75	14.73	15.71	17.14

Abacus

The abacus was one of the first calculating tools. This is a Chinese abacus, or *suan pan*. Each bead above the bar represents 5 units. Each bead below the bar represents 1 unit. Write the number shown on each abacus.

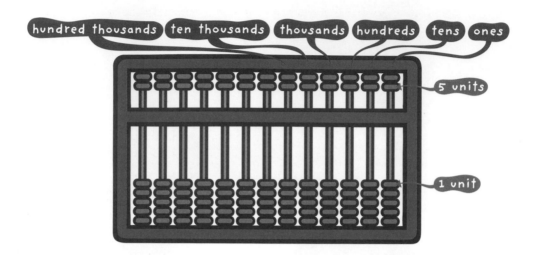

1.
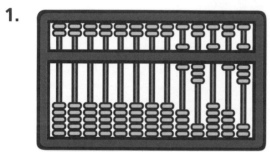

2.
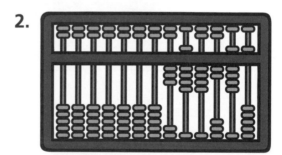

3.
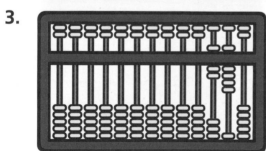

4.
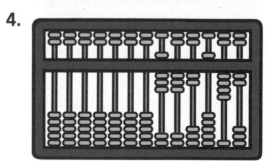

5.
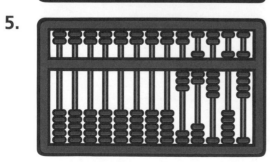

6. Draw the number 207,814 on the abacus below.

Abacus Decimals

Write the decimal shown on each abacus.

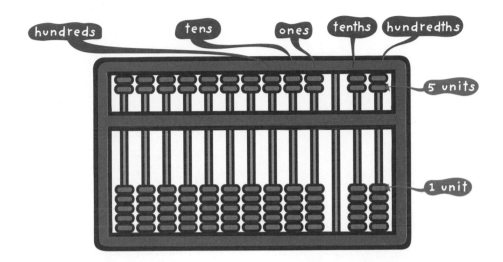

1.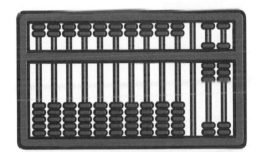

2.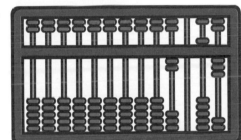

3.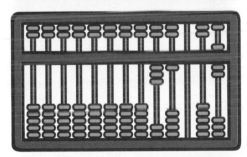

4.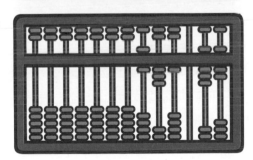

5.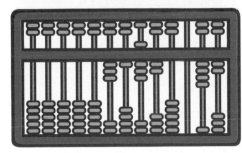

6. Draw the decimal 35,928.49 below on the abacus.

Be the Teacher

Pretend you are the teacher. This is Becky's test. Check her answers and circle the ones she answered incorrectly.

Name: Becky

1. $9\overline{)348}$ = 39 R6

2. $8\overline{)174}$ = 21 R6

3. $3\overline{)411}$ = 132

4. $5\overline{)822}$ = 164 R2

5. $8\overline{)585}$ = 73 R1

6. $4\overline{)256}$ = 55

7. $6\overline{)736}$ = 121 R4

8. $7\overline{)858}$ = 122 R4

9. $8\overline{)605}$ = 75 R5

10. $9\overline{)974}$ = 108 R3

This is the second part of Becky's test. Check her answers and circle the ones that she answered incorrectly.

Name: _Becky_____

11. 729
   × 57
   ‾‾‾‾‾
   41,552

12. 789
   × 90
   ‾‾‾‾‾
   71,010

13. 332
   × 36
   ‾‾‾‾‾
   11,952

14. 908
   × 84
   ‾‾‾‾‾
   76,270

15. 662
   × 87
   ‾‾‾‾‾
   57,681

16. 929
   × 82
   ‾‾‾‾‾
   76,178

17. 833
   × 50
   ‾‾‾‾‾
   41,650

18. 590
   × 33
   ‾‾‾‾‾
   20,060

19. 410
   × 87
   ‾‾‾‾‾
   35,670

20. 364
   × 59
   ‾‾‾‾‾
   21,417

Color the Stripes

Jessica made a mural with a pattern of stripes. She doesn't have a camera to take a picture to show you what it looks like, so she's given you these clues to figure it out. Color the mural using the clues to make a picture of what Jessica's mural looks like.

Clues:

- The stripes are red, green, yellow, and purple.

- $\frac{4}{10}$ of the stripes are green.

- $\frac{2}{10}$ of the stripes are purple.

- There are the same number of red and yellow stripes.

- None of the same colored stripes are next to each other.

- Stripes 3 and 6 are the same color.

- Stripes 2, 7, and 9 are the same color.

- Stripes 1, 2, 3, and 5 are all different colors.

- Stripe 1 is yellow.

- Stripe 5 is purple.

- The colors for stripes 6 and 8 are in alphabetical order.

1	2	3	4	5	6	7	8	9	10

Disappearing Digits

Many digits disappeared from the addition and subtraction problems below. Figure out the missing numbers and write them in the boxes.

1.
$$38,28\boxed{6}$$
$$-\ 1,\boxed{1}19$$
$$3\boxed{7},1\boxed{6}7$$

2.
$$\boxed{6}7,514$$
$$+\ \boxed{7},0\boxed{9}1$$
$$74,\boxed{6}0\boxed{5}$$

3.
$$\boxed{1}2,8\boxed{6}2$$
$$-\ \boxed{4},70\boxed{1}$$
$$8,\boxed{1}61$$

4.
$$3\boxed{2},5\boxed{8}6$$
$$-\ 5,\boxed{1}60$$
$$27,42\boxed{6}$$

5.
$$\boxed{9}\boxed{4},9\boxed{0}5$$
$$+\ 67,\boxed{3}33$$
$$\boxed{1}62,23\boxed{8}$$

6.
$$\boxed{8}\boxed{2},199$$
$$-\ \ 3,6\boxed{1}\boxed{6}$$
$$78,\boxed{5}83$$

7.
$$\boxed{7}\boxed{0},871$$
$$+\ \ 1,98\boxed{6}$$
$$72,\boxed{8}\boxed{5}7$$

8.
$$73,\boxed{2}27$$
$$-\ \boxed{9},8\boxed{2}\boxed{0}$$
$$\boxed{6}3,407$$

9.
$$\boxed{7},0\boxed{3}8$$
$$+\ 9,640$$
$$16,\boxed{6}7\boxed{8}$$

Find Your Partner!

Mrs. Cutler's class is doing a project. The class will be divided into groups of two. Mrs. Cutler gave out cards with fractions and mixed numbers. Match up the partners by drawing lines between students holding cards showing equivalent amounts.

Math Bingo

Kenny and his friends are playing bingo. A division or multiplication problem is called out, and each player has to find the answer on his or her card and put an **X** on it. The first player to have **X**s fill a whole row, column, or diagonal wins.

These are the problems that were called out (read across):

1,652 ÷ 4 =	328 × 19 =	2,079 ÷ 9 =	3,162 ÷ 6 =	2,329 × 13 =	268 × 41 =
17,970 ÷ 5 =	623 ÷ 7 =	457 × 53 =	3,927 ÷ 3 =	21,503 × 4 =	47,032 ÷ 8 =
5,166 ÷ 2 =	4,328 × 23 =	10,542 × 7 =	73 × 51 =	59,856 ÷ 8 =	32,941 × 13 =

These are Kenny and his friends' cards:

Kenny

231	12,418	89	3,723
24,221	99,544	9,021	413
995	527	7,482	428,233
5,879	4,560	10,988	5,681

Raina

527	57	6,232	7,482
428,233	5,879	5,681	231
9,021	413	73,794	2,583
89	754	86,012	12,418

Omar

99,544	17,245	754	527
5,681	413	2,583	4,560
3,594	6,232	73,794	995
57	86,012	9,021	30,277

Kristina

231	995	413	2,583
5,879	3,723	12,418	24,221
17,245	6,232	428,233	10,988
1,309	231	7,482	754

1. Who is the winner?

_____

2. What numbers were in the row, column, or diagonal of the winning player?

_____

_____

_____

_____

73

Good-bye, Multiplication!
See You Later, Division!

The multiplication and division signs in the problems below are missing. Add ✕ and ÷ signs to make each number sentence is true.

1. 8 ☐ 49 ☐ 7 = 56

2. 85 ☐ 5 ☐ 2 = 34

3. 56 ☐ 4 ☐ 39 = 546

4. 84 ☐ 50 ☐ 5 = 840

5. 36 ☐ 2 ☐ 3 ☐ 18 = 3

6. 15 ☐ 4 ☐ 3 ☐ 2 = 40

7. 2 ☐ 5 ☐ 10 ☐ 2 = 2

8. 42 ☐ 6 ☐ 5 ☐ 2 = 70

Odd and Even Subtraction

The subtraction problems below are missing numbers! Create your own subtraction problems by writing even numbers in the squares and odd numbers in the triangles.

1.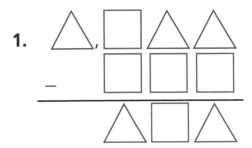

2.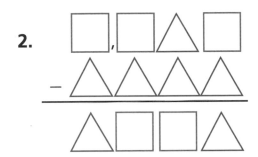

3.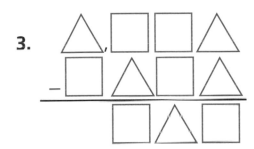

4.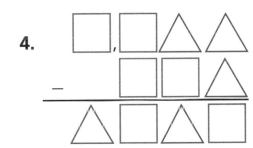

5.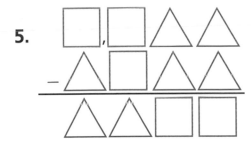

6.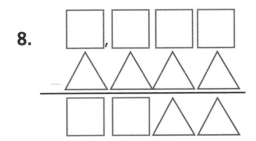

7.

8.

Ordered Pair Patterns

Write the next ordered pair in each pattern.

1. (8, 2) (12, 3) (16, 4) (20, 5) _____

2. (2, 6) (3, 9) (4, 12) (5, 15) _____

3. (3, 8) (4, 10) (5, 12) (6, 14) _____

4. (6, 17) (8, 23) (10, 29) (12, 35) _____

Each pattern above goes with an equation.
Write which pattern goes with each equation.

5. $y = 3x - 1$ _____

6. $y = 3x$ _____

7. $x = 4y$ _____

8. $y = 2x + 2$ _____

Each ordered pair goes with one of the patterns on the previous page.
Match the ordered pair to its pattern.

9. (120, 360) _____

10. (79, 160) _____

11. (144, 36) _____

12. (82, 245) _____

Write three ordered pairs that would go with each of these equations.

13. $y = 4x - 3$ _____ _____ _____

14. $y = 5x + 10$ _____ _____ _____

15. $y = 7x - 4$ _____ _____ _____

16. $y = 13x$ _____ _____ _____

Pascal's Triangle

The numbers used to make Pascal's triangle are formed by adding the two numbers directly above. The first and last number of each row is always 1. Fill in the rest of the numbers in Pascal's Triangle.

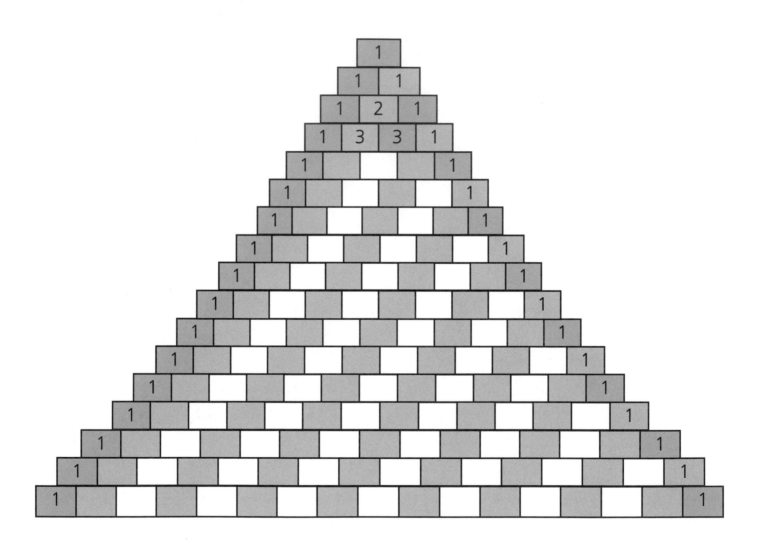

Roger's Route

Roger has a paper route that goes through the neighborhood. When you add up all the signs along his route, the total is 123.45. Use the map below to find Roger's route.

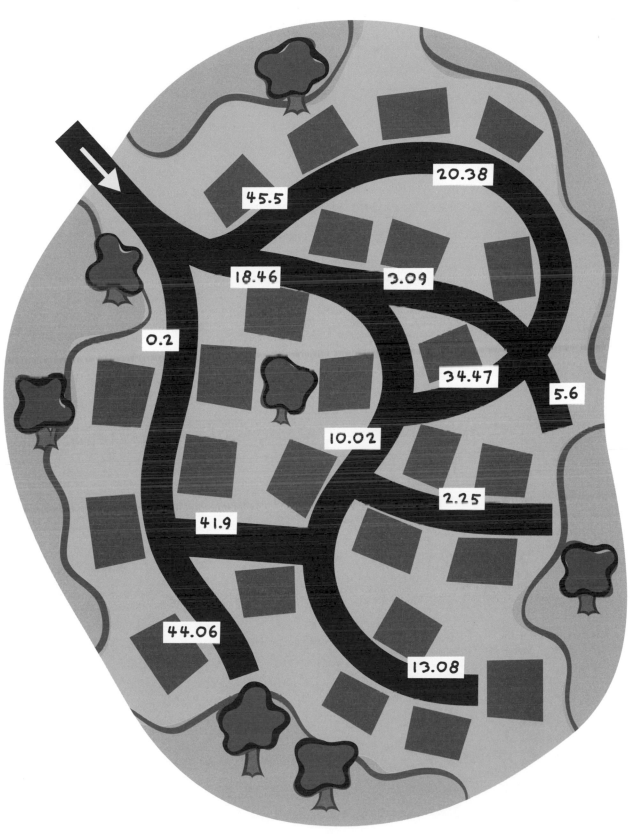

Roman Numeral Sequences

Use the information about Roman numerals in the box to complete each of the patterns below. Remember that if a smaller number is written before a larger one then you subtract them.

I = 1   C = 100
V = 5   D = 500
X = 10   M = 1,000
L = 50

Remember these shortcuts:
III = 1 + 1 + 1 = 3   XL = 50 − 10 = 40
IV = 5 − 1 = 4   CD = 500 − 100 = 400
VI = 5 + 1 = 6   CM = 1,000 − 100 = 900
IX = 10 − 1 = 9   MC = 1,000 + 100 = 1,100

1. XXXVII, XLV, LIII, LXI, _____

2. CXXI, CXXVIII, CXXXIV, CXXXIX, _____

3. MMDLX, MCCLXXX, DCXL, CCCXX, _____

4. CCCXL, MXX, DX, MDXXX, _____

5. MMMCCLXXIII, MMMCCLXXXIV, MMMCCLXXVIII, MMMCCLXXXIX,
_____

6. MMCXXXVI, MMVII, MMXLIV, MCMXV, _____

7. CCCLXII, CDXLI, DXXX, DCXXIX, _____

8. MDCXXI, MMMCCXLII, MMDCCCLXXI, MMMMMDCCXLII, _____

Taking Turns

Look at each shape in the chart. Turn each shape the given amount in a clockwise direction and draw it in the space provided. The first one has been done for you.

		90°	180°	270°	360°
1.					
2.					
3.					
4.					
5.					
6.					

Pyramid Puzzle

Patrick needs your help. He wants to stack 78 books so that each shelf would have one more book than the shelf above it. Draw a picture to show Patrick how to stack the books if his bookshelf has 12 shelves.

Rat Race

The rats are having a race to see who can get the cheese first. Color in how far each rat has gone so far.

1. $\frac{1}{2}$ of the way

2. $\frac{5}{8}$ of the way

3. $\frac{1}{8}$ of the way

4. $\frac{3}{8}$ of the way

5. $\frac{3}{4}$ of the way

Word Search

Answer each question below. Then circle the answers in the word search. The leftover letters that were not used will spell out the answer to the riddle.

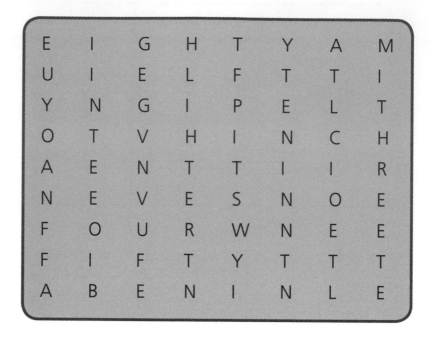

1. What is the least common multiple of 4, 5, and 10? _____

2. What is 7 and 62 hundredths rounded to the nearest whole number?

_____

3. Which of the following numbers is a prime number: 4, 5, 6, 8? _____

4. What is the number of days in a week plus the number of tails on three dogs?

_____

5. What is the greatest common factor of 18, 36, and 45? _____

6. What is 80 and 47 hundredths rounded to the nearest

whole number? _____

7. What is the number of months in a year divided by the number of eggs

in a dozen? _____

8. Which of the following numbers is a prime number: 6, 7, 8, 9, 10?

_____

9. What is the number of toes on a person times the number of tongues on five

monkeys? _____

10. What is the greatest common factor of 8, 16, and 28? _____

11. What is eighty-nine and seven tenths rounded to the nearest whole number?

_____

12. What is the number of hours in a day divided by the number of eyes on four birds?

_____

What kind of table has no legs?

___ ___ ___ ___ ___ ___ ___ ___ ___ ___ ___ ___ ___ ___

___ ___ ___ ___ ___

Unit Prices

Lizzie is going grocery shopping. Help her find the best deals by circling the better option in each problem.

1. A 1-lb bag of rice for $2.99 or a 1.5-lb bag of rice for $3.99

2. A 16-oz box of cereal for $4.50 or a 20-oz box of cereal for $5.99

3. A quart of milk for $1.39 or a half gallon of milk for $2.50

4. A package of 3 shirts for $9.99 or a package of 3 shirts for $3.00 each

5. A bag of 10 apples for $4.39 or a bag of 14 apples for $5.49

6. A box of pencils for $1.29 or 3 boxes of pencils for $4.00

7. A package of 150 sheets of paper for $1.99 or a package of 350 sheets of paper for $4.99

8. A loaf of bread for $0.99 or 3 loaves of bread for $3.29

9. A box of 4 cans of soup for $5.49 or a box of 10 cans of soup for $11.99

10. A 2-lb bag of flour for $2.29 or a 5-lb bag of flour for $5.99

Sandy's Shirt Spinner

At Sandy's Shirt Store, customers get to spin the wheel for every 10 orders they place. They can win one of three free T-shirts.

Make a spinner so that:

• About $\frac{1}{3}$ of the time, customers win a T-shirt with a puppy on it.

• Customers win a T-shirt with Sandy's store logo on it about three times as often as they win a T-shirt with a sun on it.

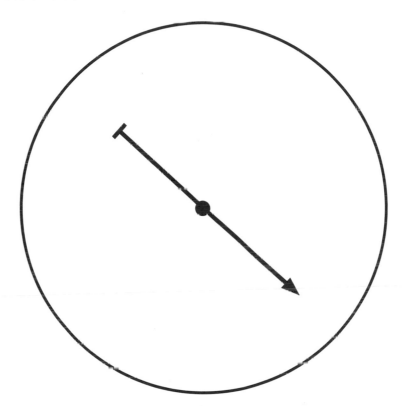

If there were 48 customers this week, fill in the tally chart with the likely results.

Puppy T-shirt	
Sandy's Store Logo T-shirt	
Sun T-shirt	

Multiplying by 25

Use the trick in the box to quickly solve the problems below.

Here's a trick for multiplying by 25:
Add 2 zeroes to the end of the number. Then divide by 4.

For example: $32,536 \times 25$
32,536 becomes 3,253,600
$3,253,600 \div 4 = 813,400$.
So, $32,536 \times 25 = 813,400$.

1. $46,597 \times 25 =$

_____

2. $68,542 \times 25 =$

_____

3. $152,695 \times 25 =$

_____

4. $365,249 \times 25 =$

_____

5. $649,724 \times 25 =$

_____

6. $4,512,365 \times 25 =$

_____

7. $8,546,328 \times 25 =$

_____

8. $25,749,865 \times 25 =$

_____

Multiplying by 125

Use the trick in the box to quickly solve the problems below.

> Here's a trick for multiplying by 125:
> Add 3 zeroes to the end of the number. Then divide by 8.
>
> For example: 541 × 125
> 541 becomes 541,000. 541,000 ÷ 8 = 67,625
> So, 541 × 125 = 67,625.

1. 458 × 125 =

_____

2. 914 × 125 =

_____

3. 1,456 × 125 =

_____

4. 5,479 × 125 =

_____

5. 42,567 × 125 =

_____

6. 84,563 × 125 =

_____

7. 451,268 × 125 =

_____

8. 965,317 × 125 =

_____

Groovy Graphs

Fill in the charts based on each equation. Use the charts to plot the points. Then draw the lines and extend them past the points you plotted on the graph paper.

$y = 3x + 2$

x	y
0	2
1	5
2	8
3	
4	
5	
6	

$y = -x + 9$

x	y
0	9
1	8
2	7
3	
4	
5	
6	

$y = 3x - 6$

x	y
0	-6
1	-3
2	0
3	
4	
5	
6	

$y = -4x + 9$

x	y
0	9
1	5
2	1
3	
4	
5	
6	

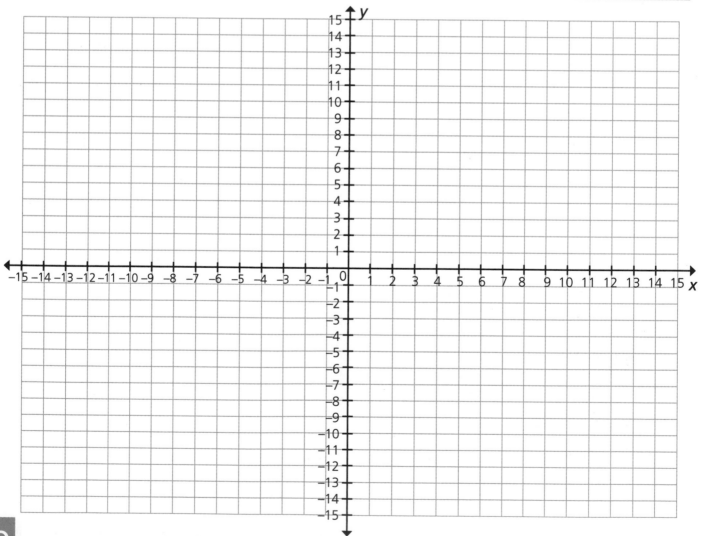

Guess and Check

Solve each problem by guessing and checking.

1. There are 80 students in fourth grade at Washington Elementary. There are six more girls than boys. How many boys and how many girls are in the fourth grade at Washington Elementary? _____

2. Polly has three coins that add up to 25 cents. What coins does she have?

_____

3. Mindy took 3 dozen cookies to school. There were peanut butter, chocolate chip, and sugar cookies. There were twice as many chocolate chip cookies as peanut butter cookies. There were 3 times as many sugar cookies as peanut butter cookies. How many of each kind of cookie did Mindy bring? _____

4. Sayid's bakery had an order for 60 cupcakes. He made twice as many chocolate cupcakes as vanilla cupcakes. He baked twice as many strawberry cupcakes as lemon cupcakes. There were 3 times as many vanilla cupcakes as lemon cupcakes. There were 3 times as many chocolate cupcakes as strawberry cupcakes. How many of each type of cupcake did Sayid make?

_____

5. Tim has 42 marbles. They are red, blue, and yellow. He has 4 more blue marbles than red marbles. He has 4 more yellow marbles than blue marbles. How many of each marble does Tim have? _____

6. Justin is thinking of a 4-digit number. The sum of its digits is 18. The last two digits are 5 times as much as the first 2 digits. The hundreds and ones places have the same digit.

_____

Funky Fractions

Circle the fraction of the shaded parts in each figure.
(Hint: sometimes the answer is in simplest form.)

1.

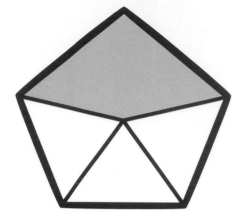

$$\frac{2}{4} \quad \frac{2}{5} \quad \frac{2}{6} \quad \frac{1}{4}$$

2.

$$\frac{1}{4} \quad \frac{2}{6} \quad \frac{2}{4} \quad \frac{1}{3}$$

3.

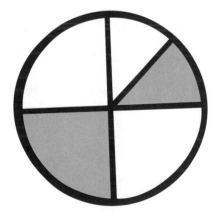

$$\frac{2}{5} \quad \frac{3}{5} \quad \frac{3}{8} \quad \frac{3}{4}$$

4.

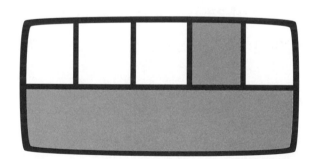

$$\frac{6}{10} \quad \frac{2}{6} \quad \frac{5}{8} \quad \frac{2}{5}$$

Boxed In

Solve the problems below. Then write the answers in the boxes so that all the numbers fit. Six answers will read left to right and the other six will read top to bottom. If an answer doesn't fit, check your work.

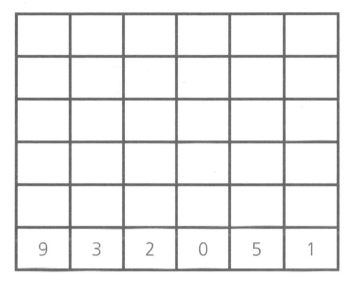

| 9 | 3 | 2 | 0 | 5 | 1 |

1. 472,591 + 459,460

=

___932,051___

2. 958,632 − 131,120

=

_____

3. 285,623 + 516,038

=

_____

4. 877,206 − 184,396

=

_____

5. 132,559 + 225,879

=

_____

6. 903,572 − 372,096

=

_____

7. 211,583 + 270,857

=

_____

8. 684,529 − 372,454

=

_____

9. 394,069 + 591,337

=

_____

10. 521,338 − 157,379

=

_____

11. 286,019 + 312,814

=

_____

12. 812,943 − 425,722

=

_____

Color Challenge

Color the shape below using only four colors. Touching shapes cannot be the same color.

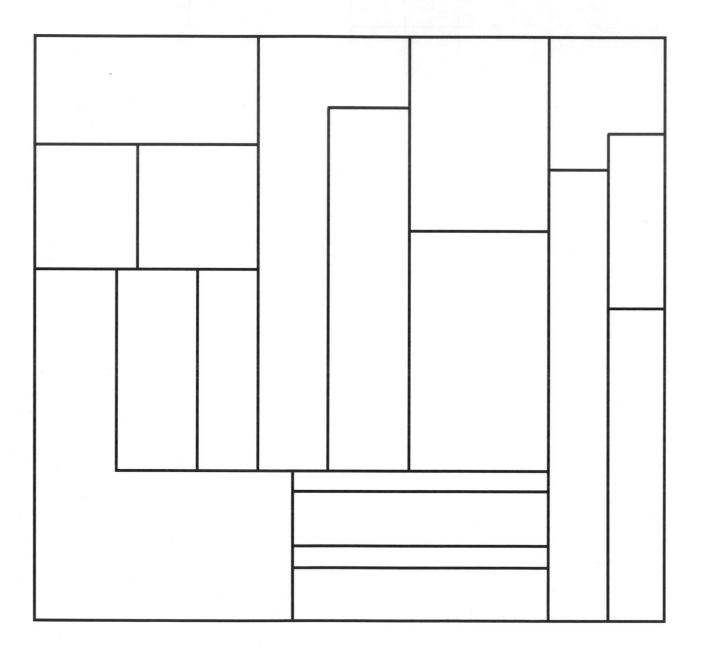

Clock Patterns

Draw the time that comes next in each pattern.

1.

2.

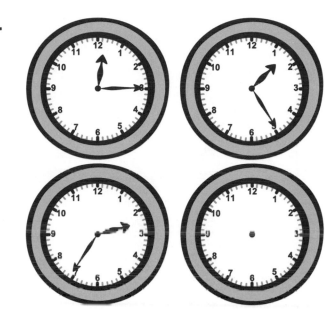

3.

4.

Congruent Figures

Color each pair of congruent figures a different color.

1.

2.

3.

4.

5.

6.

7.

8.

Now draw a congruent figure for each one that you didn't color in.

Favorite Colors

Fiona took a poll of fourth graders to see what their favorite colors are. The choices were: red, blue, yellow, and green. Fiona made this tally chart but didn't put the names of the choices. Use the clues to fill in the rest of the chart.

Clues:
- Blue was chosen three times as many as yellow.
- Red was chosen more than yellow.
- Green was chosen most often.

Colors	Tally	Number
	ЖЖ II	
	Ж I	
	IIII	
	ЖЖЖ III	

Equivalent Fractions

Solve each problem.

1. What fraction of this rectangle is shaded? _____

2. Shade these rectangles to show an equivalent
fraction of shaded sections to the fraction shown on the
rectangle in question #1. Then write the fractions on the
lines below the rectangles.

_____   _____

_____   _____

3. Divide the rectangle into 6 equal parts and shade
it to match the fraction shown in the rectangle in
question #1. Write the fraction on the line.

_____

4. What fraction of this rectangle is shaded? _____

5. Shade these rectangles to show an equivalent
fraction of shaded sections to the fraction shown
on the rectangle in question #4. Then write the
fractions on the lines below the rectangles.

_____   _____

_____   _____

Mad Multiplication

Write the product of the numbers in the circles where they overlap. The first one has been done for you.

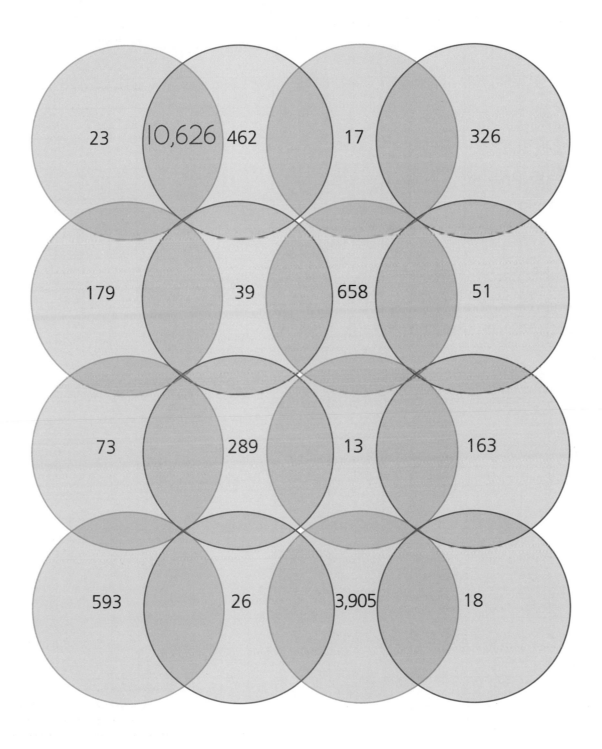

23   10,626   462   17   326

179   39   658   51

73   289   13   163

593   26   3,905   18

Possible Perimeters

Draw the possible rectangles that have the perimeter shown.

1. Draw 5 rectangles with a perimeter of 30 units.

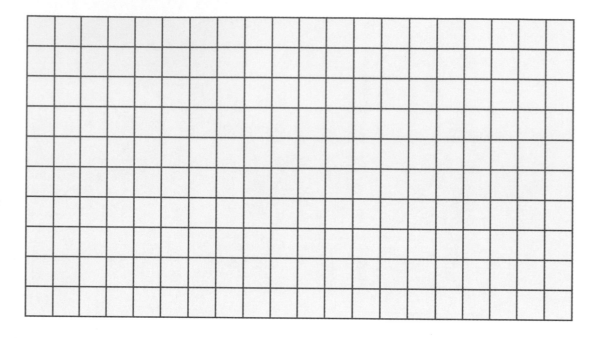

2. Draw 3 rectangles with a perimeter of 50 units.

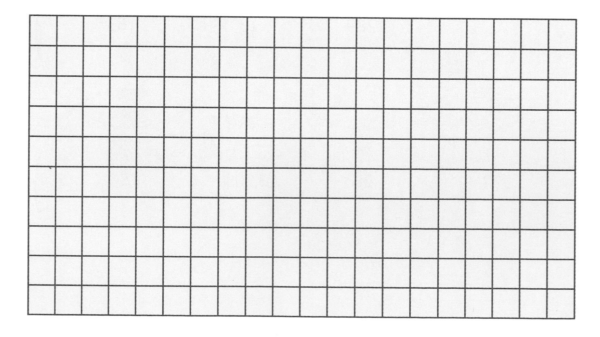

Tell Me More!

Tell what piece of information is missing for you to answer the question.

1. You want to paint your room yellow. Each wall is 80 square feet. How many gallons of paint will you need?

_____

2. Your class is having a party. You are supposed to bring cupcakes. You want to make sure there are at least 2 cupcakes for each person. If each box of cupcake mix makes 1 dozen cupcakes, how many boxes do you need to buy?

_____

3. You want to walk to your friend's house. You can walk two miles an hour. How long will it take you to get to your friend's house?

_____

4. You and your siblings are buying your mother a gift. You want to split the cost evenly. The gift costs $32.00 in total. How much does each of you have to pay?

_____

5. You volunteer at the pet shelter. Each dog gets fed 1 cup of food per 20 lbs of weight. If there are 5 dogs, how many cups of food do you need?

_____

6. You need to buy ribbon to wrap your presents. You figure out that you need 4 yards of ribbon. If each spool costs $1.99, how much will the ribbon cost?

_____

Working Backward

Solve each problem by working backward.

1. Lam brings some marbles for his friends to play with. Lam gives each of his 6 friends 4 marbles to use in the game. Lam is left with 5 marbles. How many marbles does Lam have all together? _____

2. Jenelle spends 7 dollars on a book. Then she goes home and puts half of her money in her piggy bank. Jenelle is left with 14 dollars in her pocket. How much money did Jenelle have before she bought the book? _____

3. Kevin did homework for 2 hours before watching TV for 1 hour. He then went to bed and slept for 12 hours before waking up 1 hour late for school. If school starts at 9 AM, then what time did Kevin start doing his homework? _____

4. Jya's cat had a litter of kittens. She gave 3 kittens to some of her friends at school. Her mom sold 4 kittens to friends at work. One of Jya's friends at school had to return 1 kitten because she couldn't keep it. Jya has 4 kittens left. How many kittens did Jya's cat have in the litter? _____

5. Marcus climbed to the top of a tree in his backyard. He then climbed down 6 feet before noticing a bird's nest above him. He climbed back up 3 feet to look at the bird's nest. He then climbed 9 more feet down to the ground. How high is the tree?

_____

Tricky Temperatures

Use the thermometer to answer the questions below.

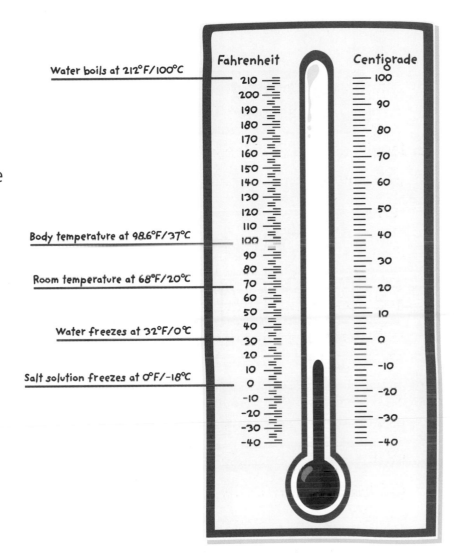

1. Which is colder, 0°F or 0°C?

_____

2. What is the temperature difference in °C between the boiling point for water and the freezing point for saltwater?

_____

3. If it is 30°F outside and the temperature drops 40°, what is the new temperature?

_____

4. If the temperature is −6°F and it rises 12°, what is the new temperature?

_____

5. How many °C must a frozen saltwater solution be raised for it to be room temperature? _____

6. It is 30°C outside. Should you go swimming or ice skating? _____

7. Which is warmer, −10°C or 10°F? _____

Nothing but Net

Fredrick made paper models of solids for a school project. He also included nets of the solids to show how he made them. But Fredrick forgot to label the nets! Can you help him label the nets with what solid it will make when folded up? Use the solids in the box.

square pyramid   rectangular prism   cone   cylinder

triangular pyramid   cube   octahedron   triangular prism

1.

_____

2.

_____

3.

_____

4.

_____

5.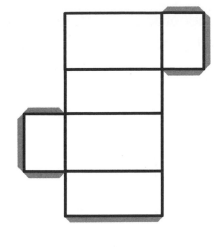

_____

6.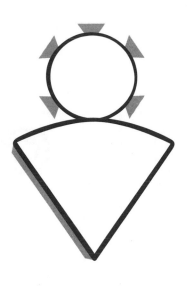

_____

7.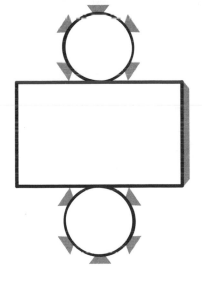

_____

8.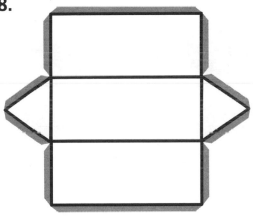

_____

Try tracing them onto another sheet of paper and folding them up to make your own solids.

Pretzel Prices

Tasty Snacks Inc., makes and sells pretzels. Twists, rods, and nuggets are all different prices. Use the diagram below to figure out how much each pretzel is worth.

 twist	+	 twist	+	 rod	= $1.77
+		+		+	
 nugget	+	 rod	+	 rod	= $1.87
+		+		+	
 rod	+	 twist	+	 rod	= $2.07
+		+		+	
 twist	+	 rod	+	 nugget	= $1.57
= $2.06		= $2.56		= $2.66	

1.  twist = _____

2.  rod = _____

3.  nugget = _____

Division Squares

Each box below has six division facts. Three run left to right and three run top to bottom. Look at the example below. Then fill in the missing numbers to complete the division boxes.

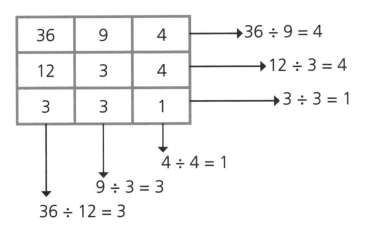

| 36 | 9 | 4 | → 36 ÷ 9 = 4
| 12 | 3 | 4 | → 12 ÷ 3 = 4
| 3 | 3 | 1 | → 3 ÷ 3 = 1

4 ÷ 4 = 1
9 ÷ 3 = 3
36 ÷ 12 = 3

1.

300	6	
10		
	6	

2.

450		90
		3
150		

3.

672	6	
84		28

4.

324		
	3	
27		9

Crazy Combos

Using the numbers on the stars, write the six-digit number described below. For each number, you must use all six digits.

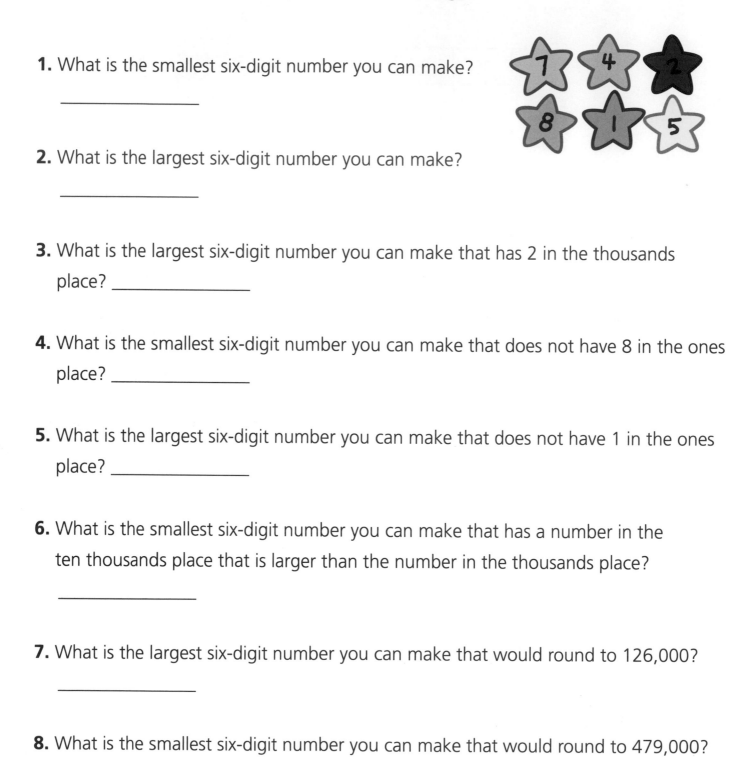

1. What is the smallest six-digit number you can make?

_____

2. What is the largest six-digit number you can make?

_____

3. What is the largest six-digit number you can make that has 2 in the thousands place? _____

4. What is the smallest six-digit number you can make that does not have 8 in the ones place? _____

5. What is the largest six-digit number you can make that does not have 1 in the ones place? _____

6. What is the smallest six-digit number you can make that has a number in the ten thousands place that is larger than the number in the thousands place?

_____

7. What is the largest six-digit number you can make that would round to 126,000?

_____

8. What is the smallest six-digit number you can make that would round to 479,000?

_____

Calculator Code

Aaron and Melanie have come up with a way to use their calculators to spell out words. All they do is type these numbers into a calculator. When they turn the calculator upside down, it spells out a word! Figure out the words that are spelled by the numbers below.

1. five thousand, three hundred six _____

2. three thousand, five hundred four _____

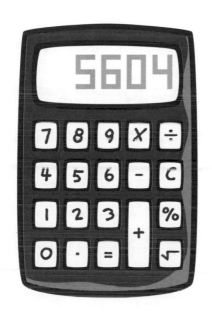

3. seven thousand, one hundred five _____

4. three thousand, forty-five _____

5. four thousand, six hundred fifteen _____

6. thirty-five thousand, seven _____

7. fifty-seven thousand, seven hundred fourteen _____

8. five hundred seventy-seven thousand, three hundred forty-five

_____

For an extra challenge, see what other words you can make with your calculator.

Decimal Pyramids

To complete the decimal pyramids, fill the bottom row of the pyramid with the numbers given. Add two adjacent numbers and put their sum in the box above them. Continue adding until you reach the top of the pyramid.

1. 10.21, 13.76, 18.45, 5.6

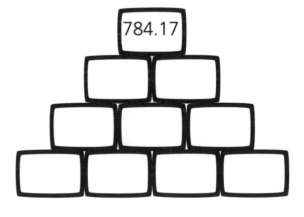

2. 17.61, 6.07, 12.52, 14.4

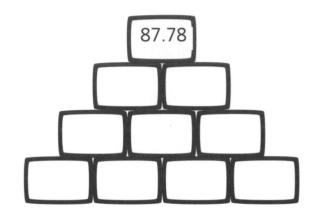

3. 116.32, 84.8, 97.14, 122.03

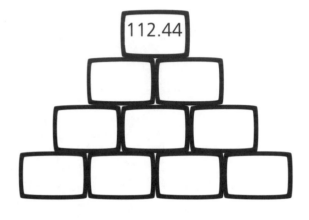

4. 183.49, 788.51, 75.6, 423.75 , 357.47

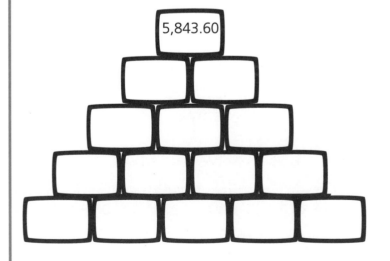

Time to Go!

Otto Octopus has as many kids as he has legs! Each child has to be somewhere at a different time today. Right now it's 9:23. Answer the questions.

1. Abby has to be at swim practice in 97 minutes. What time is that? _____

2. Billy has a baseball game in 37 minutes. What time is that? _____

3. Carly has band practice in 1 hr 7 minutes. What time is that? _____

4. Devon has guitar lessons in 2 hours and 37 minutes. What time is that?

_____

5. Ellie has a birthday party 30 minutes after Abby's practice starts. What time is that?

_____

6. Freddy's book club meets at the library 45 minutes after Billy's game starts. What time is that? _____

7. Gert is meeting her friends at the mall 1 hr 45 minutes before Devon's guitar lessons. What time is that?_____

8. Henry and Otto want to go to the movies. If they need 15 minutes to get there, what's the earliest time they can see a movie? _____

Child	Time	Child	Time
	10:00		11:00
	10:15		11:30
	10:30		12:00
	10:45	Henry	12:15

Now help Otto plan his schedule by putting the children in the order that they need to be somewhere.

Birthday Bonanza

Alan, Natalie, Rita, and Seth were each born on a different date in a different week of October (October 10, October 17, October 2, and October 26). Use the clues to figure out each person's birthday and write it on the calendar below.

Clues:
- This year, Alan's birthday will be on a Friday.
- Rita's birthday is after Alan's birthday.
- Alan's birthday is after Natalie's birthday.
- Rita's birthday is in the second half of the month.
- This year, Seth's birthday will be on a Thursday.
- Rita's birthday falls on the weekend.

	October 2	October 10	October 17	October 26
Alan				
Natalie				
Rita				
Seth				

Conversion Magic

When you convert fractions to decimals, you divide the top number of the fraction by the bottom number of the fraction. But some fractions have special patterns. See if you can find the patterns in the fractions below and convert them without dividing.

1. $\dfrac{1}{4}$ = 0.25 $\qquad$ $\dfrac{2}{4}$ = 0.50 $\qquad$ $\dfrac{3}{4}$ = _____

2. $\dfrac{1}{5}$ = 0.20 $\qquad$ $\dfrac{2}{5}$ = 0.40 $\qquad$ $\dfrac{3}{5}$ = 0.60

$\dfrac{4}{5}$ = _____

3. $\dfrac{1}{9}$ = 0.111 $\qquad$ $\dfrac{2}{9}$ = 0.222 $\qquad$ $\dfrac{3}{9}$ = 0.333

$\dfrac{4}{9}$ = _____ $\qquad$ $\dfrac{5}{9}$ = _____

$\dfrac{6}{9}$ = _____ $\qquad$ $\dfrac{7}{9}$ = _____

$\dfrac{8}{9}$ = _____

4 $\dfrac{1}{10}$ = 0.10 $\qquad$ $\dfrac{2}{10}$ = 0.20 $\qquad$ $\dfrac{3}{10}$ = _____

$\dfrac{4}{10}$ = _____ $\qquad$ $\dfrac{5}{10}$ = _____

$\dfrac{6}{10}$ = _____ $\qquad$ $\dfrac{7}{10}$ = _____

$\dfrac{8}{10}$ = _____ $\qquad$ $\dfrac{9}{10}$ = _____

5. $\dfrac{1}{11}$ = 0.0909 $\qquad$ $\dfrac{2}{11}$ = 0.1818 $\qquad$ $\dfrac{3}{11}$ = 0.2727

$\dfrac{4}{11}$ = _____ $\qquad$ $\dfrac{5}{11}$ = _____

$\dfrac{6}{11}$ = _____ $\qquad$ $\dfrac{7}{11}$ = _____

$\dfrac{8}{11}$ = _____ $\qquad$ $\dfrac{9}{11}$ = _____ $\qquad$ $\dfrac{10}{11}$ = _____

I Don't Belong Here

Five of the numbers in each row have something in common. One of them doesn't belong. Circle the number in each row that doesn't belong.

1. 500 700 273 900 200 300

2. 306 450 621 300 135 243

3. 91 126 98 81 105 84

4. 318 216 528 736 440 812

5. 876 234 148 369 172 906

6. 299 149 539 439 749 612

7. 555 222 777 123 333 111

8. 404 300 101 707 808 505

9. 122 422 222 722 999 622

10. 165 333 105 285 705 475

Look at the numbers you circled. They all have something in common. Do you know what it is? _____

Mason's computer has gone haywire! He wanted to print out some math expressions, but instead of addition, subtraction, multiplication, and division symbols, he got these strange symbols. Can you decipher which operation each symbol below represents?

1. 25 ↗ 5 ↗ 40 = 70

ㅤ↗ means _____

2. 1,200 @ 600 @ 100 = 500

ㅤ@ means _____

3. 15 : 5 : 2 − 150

ㅤ: means _____

4. 100 U 4 U 5 = 5

ㅤU means _____

Now use the operations to solve these problems.

5. 3,214 U 2 @ 7 : 3 ↗ 200 = _____

6. 34 ↗ 66 @ 5 U 10 : 4 = _____

Multiplying by 52

Use the trick to quickly solve the problems below.

Here's a trick for multiplying by 52:
1. Add 2 zeroes to the end of the number. Divide by 2.
2. Multiply the original number by 2.
3. Add Steps 1 and 2 together.

For example: $245 \times 52 =$
245 becomes 24,500. $24,500 \div 2 = 12,250$
$245 \times 2 = 490$
$12,250 + 490 = 12,740$
So, $245 \times 52 = 12,740$.

1. $537 \times 52 = $ _____

2. $965 \times 52 = $ _____

3. $1,569 \times 52 = $ _____

4. $2,454 \times 52 = $ _____

5. $52,678 \times 52 = $ _____

6. $64,853 \times 52 = $ _____

7. $236,548 \times 52 = $ _____

8. $312,659 \times 52 = $ _____

Name That Fraction!

Use the clues to find each fraction.

1. It is equivalent to $\frac{1}{4}$. The numerator and denominator add up to 15.

_____

2. It is equivalent to $\frac{1}{2}$. The denominator is 8 more than the numerator.

_____

3. It is equivalent to $\frac{2}{3}$. The denominator is odd. The numerator plus the denominator add up to less than 20. _____

4. It is equivalent to $\frac{3}{4}$. The denominator is 4 more than the numerator.

_____

5. It is equivalent to $\frac{1}{3}$. The numerator is a single-digit number. The ones digit of the numerator and denominator are equal. _____

6. It is equivalent to $\frac{1}{2}$. The numerator is the smallest 2-digit number that it could be. _____

7. It is equivalent to $\frac{1}{4}$. Both the numerator and denominator are single-digit numbers. _____

8. It is equivalent to $\frac{2}{3}$. The numerator and denominator added together equal 10. _____

On the Clock

Tina works in the payroll department at Louie's Garage. She has to figure out how many hours to pay each employee for. Use the charts to help Tina determine how many hours each employee worked.

1.

Start	End
11:15 AM	4:30 PM
5:00 PM	8:30 PM

_____ hours

2.

Start	End
7:30 AM	11:05 AM
12:10 PM	6:35 PM

_____ hours

3.

Start	End
9:25 AM	1:35 PM
2:05 PM	7:25 PM

_____ hours

4.

Start	End
12:20 PM	5:35 PM
6:00 PM	10:30 PM

_____ hours

5.

Start	End
8:45 AM	11:55 AM
12:30 PM	9:20 PM

_____ hours

6.

Start	End
10:00 AM	12:45 PM
1:50 PM	7:20 PM

_____ hours

7.

Start	End
6:35 AM	11:05 AM
12:15 PM	5:30 PM

_____ hours

8.

Start	End
7:20 AM	10:50 AM
11:45 AM	5:15 PM

_____ hours

9.

Start	End
10:55 AM	1:20 PM
2:05 PM	10:10 PM

_____ hours

10.

Start	End
5:45 AM	10:05 AM
11:00 AM	4:55 PM

_____ hours

11.

Start	End
9:45 AM	12:15 PM
1:30 PM	7:30 PM

_____ hours

12.

Start	End
6:35 AM	1:00 PM
2:00 PM	4:35 PM

_____ hours

Polygon Posters

Bryant likes to collect sports posters. His poster collection is unusual because he also likes polygons. The posters in his collection are different shapes. Use the clues and the chart below to find out which posters are in Bryant's collection. Put an **X** in a box when you eliminate something. Put an **O** in a box when you make a match.

Clues:
- The basketball poster has more than four sides.
- The soccer poster has the greatest number of angles.
- The football poster is next to the square poster.
- The hockey poster has four 90° angles.
- The baseball poster has more sides than the football poster.
- The sides of the hockey poster are equilateral.

	Hexagon	Octagon	Rectangle	Triangle	Square
Baseball					
Basketball					
Football					
Hockey					
Soccer					

Prime Time

A prime number is a whole number with exactly two factors: itself and 1. The sieve of Eratosthenes is a way to find prime numbers. Here's how it works:

1. Cross out 1. (1 is not prime.)
2. Circle 2. (2 is prime.)
3. Cross out other multiples of 2.
4. Circle 3. (3 is prime.)
5. Cross out other multiples of 3.
6. Circle 5 and 7. Cross out their other multiples.
7. The numbers left are prime. They are "caught in the sieve."

1. Use the rules above to find the prime numbers on the chart on page 121. List the prime numbers between 1 and 100.

_____

_____

_____

_____

_____

2. Why did you have to cross out numbers in steps 3, 5, and 6?

_____

1	2	3	4	5	6	7	8	9	10
11	12	13	14	15	16	17	18	19	20
21	22	23	24	25	26	27	28	29	30
31	32	33	34	35	36	37	38	39	40
41	42	43	44	45	46	47	48	49	50
51	52	53	54	55	56	57	58	59	60
61	62	63	64	65	66	67	68	69	70
71	72	73	74	75	76	77	78	79	80
81	82	83	84	85	86	87	88	89	90
91	92	93	94	95	96	97	98	99	100

More Prime Numbers

Continue to follow the rules you applied to the chart on page 121.
Once you find a prime number, cross out its multiples.

101	102	103	104	105	106	107	108	109	110
111	112	113	114	115	116	117	118	119	120
121	122	123	124	125	126	127	128	129	130
131	132	133	134	135	136	137	138	139	140
141	142	143	144	145	146	147	148	149	150
151	152	153	154	155	156	157	158	159	160
161	162	163	164	165	166	167	168	169	170
171	172	173	174	175	176	177	178	179	180
181	182	183	184	185	186	187	188	189	190
191	192	193	194	195	196	197	198	199	200

List all the prime numbers from 101 to 200.

_____

_____

_____

_____

Prime Sums

Find prime numbers that add up to the numbers shown. Use the list of prime numbers that you found on the previous pages. There may be more than one way to do each problem.

1. 12 = _____ + _____

2. 16 = _____ + _____

3. 20 = _____ + _____ or _____ + _____

4. 24 = _____ + _____ or _____ + _____ or _____ + _____

5. 34 = _____ + _____ or _____ + _____ or _____ + _____ or _____ + _____

6. 46 = _____ + _____ or _____ + _____ or _____ + _____ or _____ + _____

7. 58 = _____ + _____ or _____ + _____ or _____ + _____ or _____ + _____

8. 60 = _____ + _____ or _____ + _____ or _____ + _____ or _____ + _____ or

_____ + _____ or _____ + _____

9. 72 = _____ + _____ + _____ or _____ + _____ + _____ or

_____ + _____ + _____ or _____ + _____ + _____ or _____ + _____ + _____

10. 80 = _____ + _____ + _____ or _____ + _____ + _____ or

_____ + _____ + _____ or _____ + _____ + _____ or _____ + _____ + _____

or _____ + _____ + _____ or _____ + _____ + _____

Relay Replay

Laura, Howie, Clyde, and Maddy are on the track team. Today, they did a two-lap race. The times for the first lap were: 28.220, 28.75, 29.39, and 30.39 seconds. The times for the second lap were: 28.187, 29.72, 29.18, and 30.51 seconds. Use the clues to figure out how long it took each person to finish each lap, his or her total time, and what place each came in. Then fill in the chart with the information.

Clues:

- It took Howie approximately 30 seconds to complete the first lap.
- Laura took 33 thousandths of a second longer to finish the first lap than to complete the second lap.
- Clyde finished the second lap only 993 thousandths of a second behind the winner.
- Maddy finished the first lap only 53 hundredths of a second behind the winner.
- It took Maddy approximately 30 seconds to complete the second lap.
- Laura took a combined fifty-six and four hundred seven thousandths seconds to finish the first and second laps.

	Lap 1	Lap 2	Total Time	Place
Clyde				
Howie				
Laura				
Maddy				

Some Stamps

David, Katherine, Alexis, Mackenzie, and Nate are all members of the Stamp Club. Each has a different number of stamps (350, 319, 307, 340, and 317) in his or her collection. Use the clues to figure out how many stamps each has. Put an **X** in a box when you eliminate a number. Put an **O** in a box when you make a match.

Clues:

- Katherine has an odd number of stamps.
- The tens digit in the number of stamps that Katherine has is even.
- Neither Alexis nor Nate has an odd number of stamps.
- The hundreds digit plus the tens digit in the number of stamps Nate has is even.
- The tens digit in the number of stamps that David has is odd.
- David is not the one with 317 stamps.

	307	317	319	340	350
Alexis					
David					
Katherine					
Mackenzie					
Nate					

Riddled

Solve the riddles below.

1. First, add 8 to me. Now, if you multiply by 3, then subtract 5, you will get 25. What number am I? _____

2. First, multiply me by 4. Now, if you add 16, then divide by 2, you will get 30. What number am I? _____

3. First, divide me by 6. Now, if you add 13, then multiply by 3, you will get 51. What number am I? _____

4. First, subtract 23 from me. Now, if you multiply by 2, then add 9, you will get 57. What number am I? _____

5. First, multiply me by 7. Now, if you subtract 11, then divide by 3, you will get 15. What number am I? _____

6. First, divide me by 5. Now, if you subtract 3 and multiply by 6, then divide by 2, you will get 24. What number am I? _____

7. First, add 34 to me. Now, if you add 11, then divide by 4, you will get 21. What number am I? _____

8. First, multiply me by 9. Now, if you add 12 and divide by 11, then add 13, you will get 19. What number am I? _____

Payday

Alison, Jo, Rebecca, and Rodney work at the supermarket. This week they worked 40, 47, 38, and 37 hours. Each employee is paid at a different hourly rate ($9, $10, $11, and $15). Use the clues to figure out how many hours each employee worked this week. Also, determine each employee's hourly pay. Complete the sentences with the information.

Clues:

- This week, Jo worked the least number of hours.
- Jo earns the most amount of money per hour.
- Jo had the largest paycheck for the week.
- Rodney earns more than $9 per hour.
- Rebecca worked less than 47 hours this week.
- Alison earned $380 this week.

1. Alison worked _____ hours at _____ per hour for a total of _____.

2. Jo worked _____ hours at _____ per hour for a total of _____.

3. Rebecca worked _____ hours at _____ per hour for a total of _____.

4. Rodney worked _____ hours at _____ per hour for a total of _____.

Nina's Nifty Nines

Nina's favorite number is nine. She likes to try to name numbers using only 9s. Using addition, subtraction, multiplication, and division, can you name each number using four 9s?

Here's how she named 1 using four 9s:
$1 = 99 \div 99$ or $1 = (9 - 9) + (9 \div 9)$

1. 0

_____

2. 2

_____

3. 20

_____

4. 81

_____

5. 98

_____

6. 99

_____

7. 100

_____

8. 180

_____

Mean, Median, Mode, and Range

Find the missing number in each set using the clues provided about mean, median, mode, and/or range.

1. 15, 15, 4, 16, _____

mean = 11, median = 15

2. 22, 20, 20, 9, 19, 19, _____

mean = 19, mode = 19, 20

3. 15, 13, 27, 15, 15, _____

range = 16, mean = 19

4. 26, 16, 15, 16, 22, 15, _____

mode = 16, median = 16

5. 17, 13, 5, 12, 5, 13, _____

range = 12, mean = 11

6. 14, 22, 6, 7, 13, 19, 27, _____

mean = 17.25, median = 16.5

7. 89, 58, 82, 14, 121, 128, 61, _____

mean = 78, median = 76.5

8. 41, 11, 134, 62, 126, 145, 114, 119, 140, 51, 182, _____

range = 172, median = 122.5

9. 139, 176, 199, 87, 177, 67, 97, 67, 184, 67, 137, _____

range = 180, mean = 118

10. 182, 159, 98, 110, 105, 129, 105, 104, 184, _____

range = 86, median = 119.5

For an extra challenge, find the mean, median, mode, and/or range that wasn't given for each problem.

It's a Date!

Maya, Colby, Jasper, and Keisha are trying to plan a get-together this month. They all have very busy schedules! Use the clues to help the friends find a day that everyone has free.

Clues:

• Maya has piano lessons every other Friday starting the 4th.
• Colby has baseball games every Saturday.
• Jasper helps his grandmother on Tuesdays and Thursdays.
• Keisha will be away on vacation for seven days starting the 21st.
• Maya and Jasper study together every Monday.
• Colby has baseball practice on Wednesdays.
• Jasper has tickets to the basketball game the first and third Sundays of the month.
• Keisha can't meet on the 13th.

S	M	T	W	TH	F	S
		1	2	3	4	5
6	7	8	9	10	11	12
13	14	15	16	17	18	19
20	21	22	23	24	25	26
27	28	29	30	31		

What day does everyone have free? _____

Tricky Place Value

Write the 6-digit numbers that are described below.

1. four hundred thirty-two thousand + thirty-six hundred = _____

2. three hundred fifty-one thousand + one hundred + eighteen hundred seventeen =

_____

3. seven hundred twenty-four thousand + two hundred thousand + thirty-one =

_____

4. five hundred eleven thousand + seventy-two hundred + sixty-seven =

_____

5. two hundred nineteen thousand + three hundred thousand + forty-six =

_____

6. six hundred eighty-three thousand + eighty-seven hundred + fifty-four =

_____

7. one hundred fifty-seven thousand + twenty-eight hundred + fourteen =

_____

8. seven hundred thirty-eight thousand + forty-two hundred + seven =

_____

9. three hundred nineteen thousand + five hundred thousand + eleven =

_____

10. four hundred twenty-nine thousand + thirty-four hundred + ninety-eight =

_____

Recycling Rescue

Mrs. Finch's class, Mr. Bartoli's class, Miss Johnson's class, and Mrs. Brown's class collected items to be recycled. Each class collected a different number of magazines (20, 23, 24, and 29) and a different number of cans (112, 129, 139, and 107). Use the clues to figure out how many magazines and cans each class recycled. Then fill in the chart with the information.

Clues:

- Miss Johnson's class recycled the most number of cans.
- Mrs. Finch's class recycled more than 25 magazines.
- Mr. Bartoli's class recycled less than 120 cans.
- Mrs. Finch's class recycled 78 more cans than the number of magazines they recycled.
- If the number of magazines Mrs. Brown's class recycled was doubled, they would have recycled 48 magazines.
- Miss Johnson's class recycled the least number of magazines.

Teacher	Magazines Recycled	Cans Recycled

Pedro's Program

Pedro wrote a computer program that solves division problems and tells you the remainder. He's not sure that he coded it correctly. Fill in the answers to the problems in each table so that Pedro can use it to check his program.

1.

⬡ ÷ 9 = ▲ R ⬤

⬡	▲	⬤
134	14	8
243		
598		
997		
1,837		
6,358		

2.

⬡ ÷ 7 = ▲ R ⬤

⬡	▲	⬤
359	51	2
638		
796		
864		
1,638		
9,374		

Triangle Decimals

Put a number in each circle so that the sum of each side of the triangle is equal to the number in the middle. Use the numbers in the box for each problem, and use them only once.

1. (2.61, 4.46, 4.92, 5.98, 7.83, 8.29)

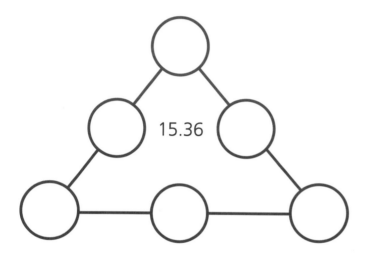

2. (3.79, 4.1, 6.84, 7.15, 7.21, 10.26)

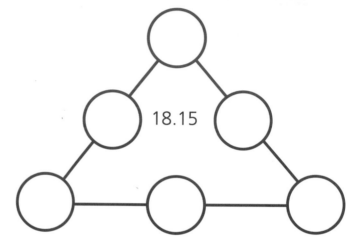

3. (1.42, 1.43, 1.44, 1.45, 1.47, 1.49)

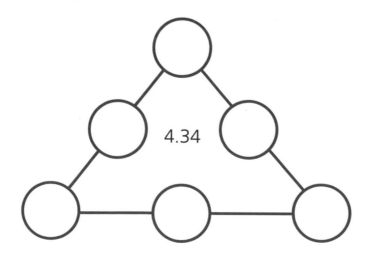

St. Ives

Laina was reading a book of nursery rhymes to her little brother. When she got to the one called "As I Was Going to St. Ives," it made her think. This is the beginning of the nursery rhyme:

> *As I was going to St. Ives*
> *I met a man with seven wives*
> *And every wife had seven sacks*
> *And every sack had seven cats*
> *And every cat had seven kittens*

Laina thought, "What if every kitten had three mice and every mouse had two pieces of cheese? How many pieces of cheese would that be altogether?" Can you figure it out for Laina?

Here is the new rhyme:

> *As I was going to St. Ives*
> *I met a man with seven wives*
> *And every wife had seven sacks*
> *And every sack had seven cats*
> *And every cat had seven kittens*
> *And every kitten had three mice*
> *And every mouse had two pieces of cheese*

How many pieces of cheese are there? Show your work. _____

The Science Fair

Nona, Tracy, and Keenan were the winners of the science fair. Use the clues to find out what project each child did and which place each one came in. Then fill in the chart with the information.

Clues:

- Keenan did not finish third.
- The first-place winner made an ant farm.
- Tracy's project is not the volcano.
- Nona finished before Keenan.
- Keenan finished before the person who raised sea monkeys.

Child	Place	Project

Shake Things Up

Mr. Anderson, Ms. Bartleby, Mr. Coleman, Mrs. D'Agostino, Miss Engers, Mr. Finch, Mr. Garero, Ms. Henderson, Mr. Ichiro, and Mrs. Jiminez arrive at Town Hall for the city council meeting. Upon entering the room, every person shakes every other person's hand.

How many handshakes are there? _____

Make a list of all the handshakes.

_____

_____

_____

_____

_____

_____

_____

_____

_____

_____

_____

_____

_____

_____

Peter's Pet Palace

Pam went to Peter's Pet Palace to buy some things for her pet parakeet, Polly. When Pam asked Peter for the price on some products, he replied with these riddles. Help Pam solve the price puzzles.

1. The price of the parakeet park playpen is more than the value of 48 quarters but less than the value of 130 dimes. The cents cannot be made using only quarters. The numbers in the price are 7, 5, 2, and 1. How much does the playpen cost? _____

2. The price of the parakeet toy is more than the value of 1 five-dollar bill. The numbers in the price are 2, 6, and 7. You can make the cents with only 2 coins. How much does the parakeet toy cost? _____

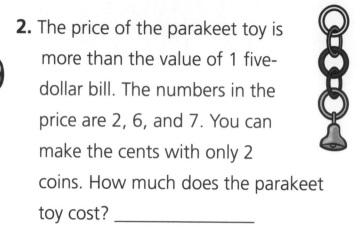

3. The price of the parakeet perch is less than the value of 1 five-dollar bill. The numbers in the price are 3, 4, and 8. The smallest number of coins you can use to make the cents is 7. How much does the parakeet perch cost? _____

4. The price of the bird swing can be made with 2 bills. It is less than the value of a five-dollar bill. The cents can be made using 2 dimes, 3 quarters, and 4 pennies. How much does the swing cost? _____

5. How much money does Pam need to buy everything? _____

6. If Pam gives Peter a 20-dollar bill and a 10-dollar bill, how much change will she get back? _____

Number Line Riddle

Write each letter in the space above the number that matches its place on the number line. Keep in mind that some fractions will need to be converted to mixed numbers. When you are done, you will see the answer to the riddle.

How many zeroes does a googol have?

$\dfrac{1}{10}$ \qquad $\dfrac{7}{10}$ \quad 1.5 \quad $\dfrac{3}{2}$ \quad 0.7 \quad $\dfrac{6}{4}$ \quad $\dfrac{8}{8}$ \qquad 0.75 \quad 0.1 \quad 1.75

$\dfrac{3}{2}$ \quad 1.25 \quad 0.5 \quad $\dfrac{3}{4}$ \quad $\dfrac{19}{10}$ \quad $\dfrac{5}{4}$ \quad $\dfrac{1}{4}$ \quad 1.6 \quad $\dfrac{2}{4}$ \quad $\dfrac{1}{4}$

$\dfrac{8}{4}$ \quad $\dfrac{5}{10}$ \quad $\dfrac{16}{10}$ \quad $\dfrac{12}{8}$ \quad $\dfrac{1}{2}$ \quad $\dfrac{7}{4}$.

Parentheses Power

Add parentheses to each problem to make the equation true. More than one set may be needed. Remember that to solve a problem, you must first perform operations inside the parentheses, then multiplication left to right, then addition and subtraction left to right.

Example: $12 - 6 + 4 = 2 \longrightarrow 12 - (6 + 4) = 2$

1. $7 + 8 \times 9 + 4 = 139$

2. $6 \times 7 + 26 - 19 + 4 = 45$

3. $31 + 8 \times 2 = 78$

4. $3 + 4 \times 7 + 309 - 3 \times 3 = 349$

5. $17 \times 10 + 9 + 8 \div 4 = 325$

6. $12,942 - 42 \div 5 = 2,580$

7. $2,646 \div 14 \times 7 - 5 = 378$

8. $429 \times 3 - 168 \div 4 - 2 = 1,203$

9. $80 + 19 + 21 \div 10 = 12$

10. $3,729 + 1,271 \div 2 + 2 + 1 = 1,000$

Phone Code

Each of the words below is a code for a number. Look at the letters that correspond to each number on the phone. Add the numbers together to crack the code for each word.

1. climate   _____

2. volcano   _____

3. explore   _____

4. perform   _____

5. relieve   _____

6. manager   _____

7. slumber   _____

8. knuckle   _____

9. thicket   _____

10. recover   _____

Round and Round

Use the numbers in the box below to answer the following questions. The same number cannot be used more than once in a number. All numbers will be decimals.

$$5, 1, 8, 2, 9, 4, 6$$

1. Write all of the three-digit numbers that can be rounded to 2.6. _____

2. Write all of the two-digit numbers that can be rounded to 9.0. _____

3. Write all of the three-digit numbers that can be rounded to 1.8. _____

4. Write all of the three-digit numbers that can be rounded to 22.0. _____

5. Write the largest three-digit number that can be rounded to 5.9. _____

6. Write the 2 largest two-digit numbers that can be rounded to 7.0.

_____

7. Write 3 three-digit numbers that can be rounded to 59.0. _____

8. Write the smallest three-digit number that can be rounded to 8.5.

_____

9. Write 3 two-digit numbers that can be rounded to 2.0. _____

10. Write the smallest two-digit number that can be rounded to 1.0. _____

Tangram Fun

Tangrams are puzzles that were invented in China a long, long time ago. They use the seven shapes in the square to make other pictures. Answer the questions below using the tangram puzzle shown.

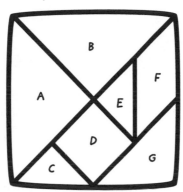

1. Name 2 pairs of shapes that could each form a triangle. _____

2. Which 4 shapes could you use to make a triangle? _____

3. Which shapes could be used to make a pentagon? _____

4. Which 5 shapes could you use to make a rectangle? _____

5. What shape can A and G make? _____

6. How can you use all of the shapes to make a rectangle? Draw a picture.

Tenths and Hundredths

Write a fraction and a decimal to answer each question.

1. What fraction of the shape is red?

_____ _____

2. What fraction of the shape is blue?

_____ _____

3. What fraction of the shape is yellow?

_____ _____

4. What fraction of the shape is green?

_____ _____

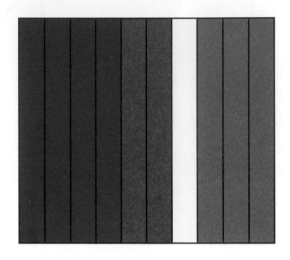

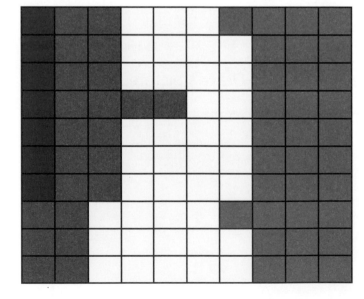

5. What fraction of the shape is red?

_____ _____

6. What fraction of the shape is blue?

_____ _____

7. What fraction of the shape is yellow?

_____ _____

8. What fraction of the shape is green?

_____ _____

Twelve Trios

To complete this page, circle sets of three numbers that add up to 12. Each number can be circled only once. You cannot cross another line. You have to use all the numbers.

4	6	1	9	3
2	4	2	2	7
4	5	3	4	4
1	7	4	2	4
0	8	6	5	3
4	1	9	2	4

Area Ace

Megan is making a rectangular garden. She wants it to be 90 square units, but no side can be longer than 20 units or shorter than 5 units. Draw 3 different ways Megan can make her garden.

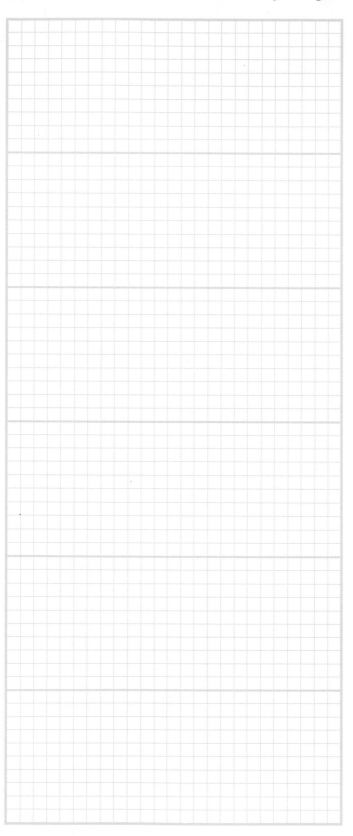

Coin Collections

Shelly, Sophie, Tyler, Hal, and Perlin collect coins. They each brought their coins to show each other. Tyler has nickels, Shelly has pennies, Sophie has half-dollars, Perlin has quarters, and Hal has dimes. Use the clues to figure out how many coins each student has and how much money it adds up to. Then fill in the chart with the information.

Clues:

- Sophie has five more coins than Shelly.
- Tyler has 10 more coins than Hal.
- Perlin, Hal, and Tyler have $7.85 worth of coins altogether.
- Perlin has 15 more coins than Hal.
- Shelly's coins are worth $16.71 less than Sophie's coins.

	Type of Coin	Number of Coins	Total Amount
Shelly	**pennies**		
Sophie	**half-dollars**		
Tyler	**nickels**		
Hal	**dimes**		
Perlin	**quarters**		

Complex Areas

Find the area of these figures. (Hint: first, break each down into shapes you know. Then add the area of those figures to find the total area.)

1.

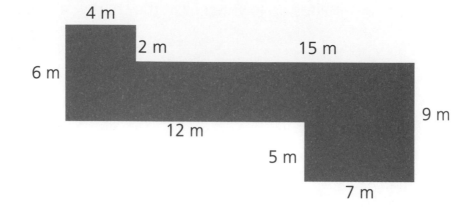

2.

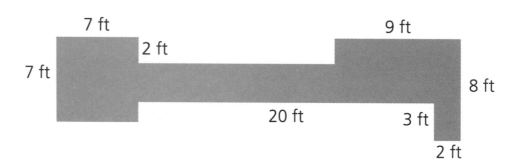

3.

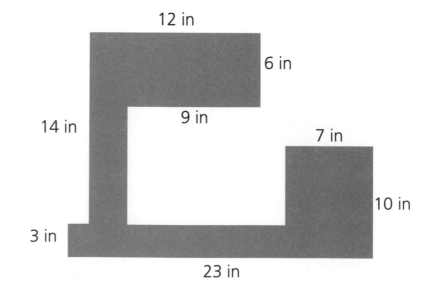

4.

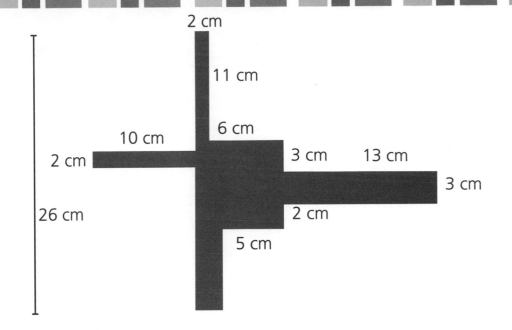

2 cm

11 cm

6 cm

10 cm

2 cm

3 cm   13 cm

3 cm

26 cm

2 cm

5 cm

_____

5.

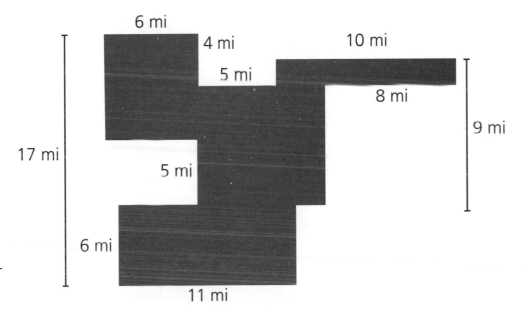

6 mi

4 mi   10 mi

5 mi

8 mi

17 mi

9 mi

5 mi

6 mi

11 mi

_____

6.

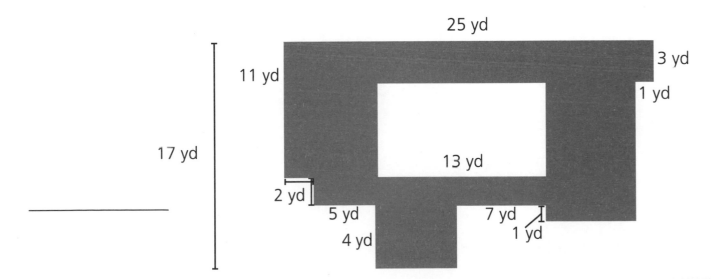

25 yd

11 yd   3 yd

1 yd

17 yd

13 yd

2 yd

5 yd   7 yd   1 yd

4 yd   1 yd

_____

Digit Dilemmas

Use the numbers in the boxes to make problems using the clues. Each number can be used only once per problem, and all the numbers must be used.

(1, 2, 3, 4, 5)

1. Make a 3-digit by 2-digit multiplication problem. The product is 3,335.

_____

2. Make a 4-digit by 1-digit division problem with a quotient of 1,328.

_____

3. Make a 4-digit by 1-digit multiplication problem. The product is 9,062.

_____

4. Make a 4-digit by 1-digit division problem. The quotient is 508.

_____

5. Put the correct operation signs in between these numbers to get an answer of 10 using the order of operations.

1 _____ 2 _____ 3 _____ 4 _____ 5 = 10

(5, 6, 7, 8, 9)

6. Make a 3-digit by 2-digit multiplication problem with a product of 60,075.

_____

7. Make a 4-digit by 1-digit division problem with a quotient of 747. _____

Division Dilemmas

Figure out the number being described in each riddle.

1. When you divide me by 2, you get 6 with a remainder of 1. _____

2. When you divide me by 7, you get 5 with a remainder of 2. _____

3. When you divide me by 10, you get 50 with a remainder of 8. _____

4. When you divide me by 30, you get 9 with a remainder of 15. _____

5. When you divide me by 46, you get 2 with a remainder of 1. _____

6. When you divide me by 84, you get 5 with a remainder of 51. _____

7. When you divide me by 9, you get 856 with a remainder of 3. _____

8. When you divide me by 8, you get 2,901 with a remainder of 7. _____

Ally's Aquarium

Ally runs a tropical fish store. Ally's tanks have four types of items: fish, snails, plants, and rocks. Each tank has a different number of each item. Using the clues provided, fill in how many of each item is in each tank.

1. There are 14 items in the tank. There are 4 times as many fish as there are plants. The number of snails and rocks is the same. Fish _____ Snails _____ Plants _____ Rocks _____

2. There are 17 items in the tank. There are 5 more snails than rocks. More than half the tank is plants. Fish _____ Snails _____ Plants _____ Rocks _____

3. There are 12 items in the tank. There are half as many plants as there are rocks. There are 5 times as many fish as there are snails. Fish _____ Snails _____ Plants _____ Rocks _____

4. There are 18 items in the tank. There are 3 more fish than there are snails. There is 1 more rock than there are plants. Fish _____ Snails _____ Plants _____ Rocks _____

5. There are 22 items in the tank. There are 3 times as many snails as there are rocks. More than half of the tank is snails and rocks. There are 4 more plants than there are fish. There are an equal number of rocks and fish. Fish _____ Snails _____ Plants _____ Rocks _____

6. There are 15 items in the tank. There are 9 more fish than there are plants. There are more snails than rocks. Fish _____ Snails _____ Plants _____ Rocks _____

Follow the Rules

Fill in the missing numbers and rules to make each problem correct.

1. _____ ➡ 50 ➡ _____ ➡ 200 ➡ 400

Rule: ➡ = × 2

2. 29 ➡ _____ ➡ 63 ➡ 80 ➡ _____

Rule: ➡ = + 17

3. 480 ➡ 240 ➡ 120 ➡ 60 ➡ 53 ➡ 46

Rule: ➡ = _____   ➡ = _____

4. 620 ➡ 570 ➡ 520 ➡ _____ ➡ _____ ➡ 510

Rule: ➡ = _____   ➡ = _____

5. 60 ➡ _____ ➡ _____ ➡ 575 ➡ _____ ➡ 645

Rule: ➡ = × 3   ➡ = _____

6. 5 ➡ 25 ➡ 40 ➡ 200 ➡ _____ ➡ _____

Rule: ➡ = _____   ➡ = + 15

Favorite Subjects

Hanna, Tamoay, Stacey, and Desmond are students. One is in second grade, one is in third grade, one is in fourth grade, and one is in fifth grade. Each of the students has a different favorite subject in school. Use the clues to match each student with his or her favorite subject and the grade that each is in.

Clues:

- The fifth-grade student's favorite subject is reading.
- Tamoay is in a higher grade than Desmond and Hanna.
- Math is the favorite subject for either the second or third-grade student.
- Desmond is in a higher grade than Hanna and Stacey.
- In the second grade, Hanna's favorite subject was art. Now, she prefers a different subject.
- Stacey is in a lower grade than Tamoay.
- Science is not Hanna's or Tamoay's favorite subject.
- There is another subject that Hanna and Desmond enjoy more than art.

1. What grade is Hanna in? _____ What is her favorite subject in school?
_____

2. What grade is Tamoay in? _____ What is his favorite subject in school?
_____

3. What grade is Stacey in? _____ What is her favorite subject in school?
_____

4. What grade is Desmond in? _____ What is his favorite subject in school?
_____

Daily Data

The Weather Club at your school recorded these temperatures for last week.
Use the chart to answer the questions below.

RECORDED TEMPERATURES

DAY	HIGH	LOW
SUNDAY	86°F	68°F
MONDAY	84°F	64°F
TUESDAY	83°F	65°F
WEDNESDAY	81°F	66°F
THURSDAY	82°F	65°F
FRIDAY	85°F	69°F
SATURDAY		

1. Someone spilled water on the chart, and Saturday can't be read. But the club members remember that the mean high temperature for the week was 84°F and the mean low temperature for the week was 66°F. What are the high and low temperatures for Saturday? _____

2. What was the temperature range for each day?

Day	Sun	Mon	Tues	Wed	Thurs	Fri	Sat
Range							

3. What was the mean temperature for the week? _____

4. What was the mean temperature for each day?

Day	Sun	Mon	Tues	Wed	Thurs	Fri	Sat
Mean							

Carpet Costs

Jess has a summer job working at his uncle's carpet store. Customers brought in the drawings below of their rooms. Help Jess determine how much it will cost to carpet each room based on the price per square foot given.

1.

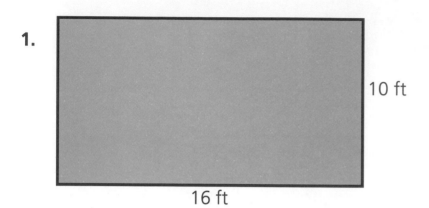

10 ft

16 ft

$8.50 per square foot

_____

2.

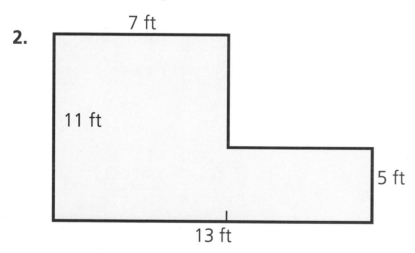

7 ft

11 ft

5 ft

13 ft

$7.75 per square foot

_____

3.

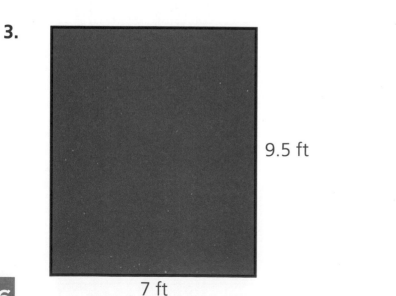

9.5 ft

7 ft

$8.39 per square foot

_____

4.

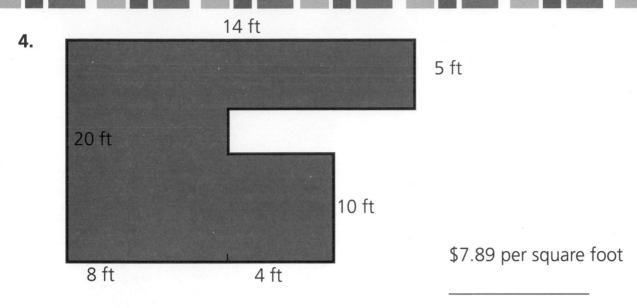

14 ft

5 ft

20 ft

10 ft

8 ft   4 ft

$7.89 per square foot

_____

5.

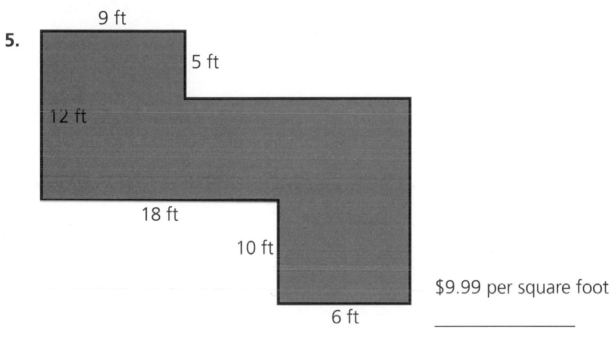

9 ft

5 ft

12 ft

18 ft

10 ft

$9.99 per square foot

6 ft

_____

6.

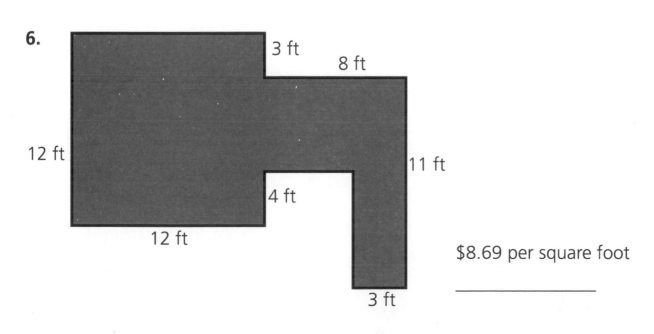

3 ft

8 ft

12 ft

11 ft

4 ft

12 ft

$8.69 per square foot

3 ft

_____

Multiplication Points

Each letter in the chart below is worth the amount given. Multiply each letter's value to find out how many points each word below is worth.

A = 1	H = 8	O = 15	V = 22
B = 2	I = 9	P = 16	W = 23
C = 3	J = 10	Q = 17	X = 24
D = 4	K = 11	R = 18	Y = 25
E = 5	L = 12	S = 19	Z = 26
F = 6	M = 13	T = 20	
G = 7	N = 14	U = 21	

1. pace _____

2. wide _____

3. vice _____

4. grief _____

5. cake _____

6. reach _____

7. nice _____

8. dance _____

What's the Best Deal?

Olivia loves a good deal. She sees these things for sale at the grocery store. Help her choose the items that will save her money.

1. The orange juice comes in a 1-pint bottle for $.89, a 2-quart bottle for $3.39, and a 1-gallon bottle for $6.99. Which is the best deal and why?

_____

2. The potatoes come in bags of different weights. There is a 1.5-lb bag for $2.49, a 3-lb bag for $4.69, and a 5-lb bag for $7.99. Which is the best deal and why?

_____

3. Olivia wants to buy some ribbon to decorate her room. She finds that a 2-yd roll costs $2.29, a 4-ft roll costs $1.39, and a 24-in roll costs $1.19. Which is the best deal and why?

_____

4. Olivia needs some paper towels. She sees that a 12-pack of 150-sheet rolls of paper towels is $1.79. An 8-pack of 200-sheet rolls of paper towels is $2.49. A 10-pack of 100-sheet rolls of paper towels is $1.29. Which is the best deal and why?

_____

5. Olivia finds that her favorite oatmeal is on sale. There is a 1-lb 8-oz box for $3.19, a 14-oz box for $2.89, and a 10-oz box for $2.49. Which is the best deal and why?

_____

6. Packs of juice of different sizes are all on sale. One pack is 10 6-oz bottles for $4.39. Another pack is 8 7-oz bottles for $4.19. The last pack is 6 12-oz bottles for $4.49. Which is the best deal and why?

_____

Color Parts

Color the figures so they match the fractions below.

1. blue + red = $\frac{2}{6}$

yellow + green = $\frac{4}{6}$

yellow + red = $\frac{2}{6}$

yellow + blue = $\frac{2}{6}$

2. orange + purple = $\frac{5}{9}$

red − purple = $\frac{2}{9}$

3. yellow + blue + orange = green

yellow + blue = $\frac{3}{10}$

yellow + orange = $\frac{4}{10}$

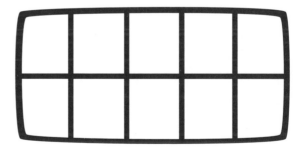

4. yellow + purple = blue + purple

blue + blue = $\frac{4}{5}$

Magic Squares

In a magic square, the sum along each row, column, and diagonal is the same. Use the magic sum for each square to complete the magic squares.

1. Magic sum = 34

	15	14	4
12		7	
8	10		5
13		2	16

2. Magic sum = 94

	5	23	44
19		15	9
35	17		31
	21	45	

3. Magic sum = 73

21		43	4
9	14		23
31		2	
	24		36

4. Magic sum = 81

	5		12
35		8	
3	57		7
4		34	26

Color the Fractions

Color the figures according to the clues. No part mentioned is equal to zero.

1.

The blue part is the largest.
The red part and the green part are equal.

2.

The black part is half the size of the yellow part.
The red part is the largest.

3.

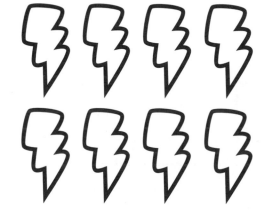

There are 3 more blue parts than there are black parts.
There are twice as many green parts as there are white parts.

4.

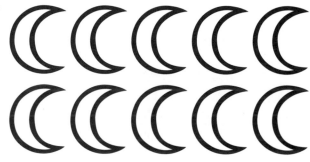

The yellow part is equal to the green part.
Two times the orange part is less than the red part.
The red part is more than all other parts combined.
The green part is half of the orange part.

In and Out

Find the rule for each function and use it to fill in the missing numbers. Write each rule in the form of an equation.

1.

Input a	Output b
5	12
15	4
3	
4	15
30	2
	60
12	5

Rule: _____

2.

Input c	Output d
17	28
28	
37	48
	65
69	80
73	
87	98

Rule: _____

3.

Input e	Output f
9	26
13	
16	19
	9
28	7
30	
	3

Rule: _____

4.

Input g	Output h
12	84
18	
29	203
	238
59	413
	497
83	

Rule: _____

Birthday Bank

On Billy's first birthday, he received $10. Every year after that he got $20 more than the year before. He has saved all the birthday money he has gotten over the years. Fill in the chart that has been started to find the answers to the questions below.

Birthday	Amount Received	Total
1	$10	$10
2	$30	$40
3	$50	$90

1. How old will Billy be before he has saved $1,000? _____

2. How old will Billy be before he has saved $4,000? _____

3. How old will Billy be before he has saved $9,000? _____

4. How old will Billy be before he has saved $16,000? _____

Awesome Arrays

Solve the problems below.

1. Pedro has 24 cars. He wants to arrange them in different groups. Write multiplication problems to show the 8 different ways that Pedro can group his cars.

_____   _____

_____   _____

_____   _____

_____   _____

2. Melissa has 48 magnets. She wants to arrange them in different groups on the refrigerator. Write multiplication problems to show the 10 different ways that Melissa can group the magnets.

_____   _____

_____   _____

_____   _____

_____   _____

_____   _____

3. Elisa has 72 rocks. Write multiplication problems to show the 12 different ways that Elisa can arrange her rocks.

_____   _____

_____   _____

_____   _____

_____   _____

_____   _____

_____   _____

4. The school wants to make a collage of all the students in the fourth grade. There are 120 students. Write multiplication problems to show the 16 different groups of students that can be shown.

_____   _____

_____   _____

_____   _____

_____   _____

_____   _____

_____   _____

_____   _____

_____   _____

Pete's Puzzling Pattern

Tina's older brother Pete gave her this puzzle to solve. Pete says that there is an easy way to find the sum of any three diagonal numbers by looking at the middle number. Can you help Tina figure it out?

+	1	2	3	4	5	6	7	8	9
1	2	3	4	5	6	7	8	9	10
2	3	4	5	6	7	8	9	10	11
3	4	5	6	7	8	9	10	11	12
4	5	6	7	8	9	10	11	12	13
5	6	7	8	9	10	11	12	13	14
6	7	8	9	10	11	12	13	14	15
7	8	9	10	11	12	13	14	15	16
8	9	10	11	12	13	14	15	16	17
9	10	11	12	13	14	15	16	17	18

1. Tina was looking at these three numbers:

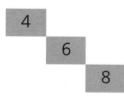

She found the sum to be 18. How can you get 18 from looking at the middle number? _____

2. Does the pattern work for these diagonal numbers? _____

9
11
13

3. Will it work for any 3 diagonal numbers? _____

Shape Substitutes

Each of the three shapes below represents a whole number from 1 to 50. Find the values for each shape based on the equations.

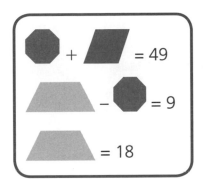

1. ▰ = _____   **2.** ⬣ = _____

Now use those values to solve these equations. Don't forget the order of operations!

3. ⬣ + ▰ × ⬣ = _____

4. ▰ + ▰ − ⬢ ÷ ⬣ = _____

5. ⬣ × ▰ + ⬢ = _____

6. ⬢ + ⬣ ÷ ⬣ × ▰ + ⬢ = _____

7. ▰ + ⬣ × ⬢ − ▰ − ⬣ = _____

8. ⬢ + ▰ × ⬣ − ⬣ × ⬢ = _____

Party Time

Amita is having a party. She wants to serve punch, cupcakes, and veggie pizza. Amita has $60.00 to spend. Twenty-four people are coming to the party. She has to have enough food and drink for everyone to have at least one serving of each item. The recipes below show the ingredients needed for the things Amita wants to serve.

Recipe

Party Punch
(serves 10)

1 liter lemon-lime soda
1 pint orange sherbet
1 quart vanilla ice cream

Recipe

Cupcakes
(serves 12)

1 package of
cupcake mix

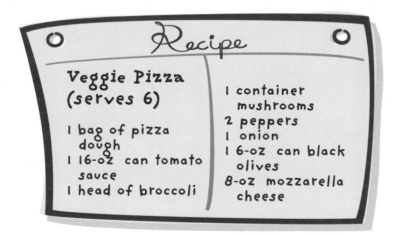

Recipe

Veggie Pizza
(serves 6)

1 bag of pizza dough
1 16-oz can tomato sauce
1 head of broccoli

1 container mushrooms
2 peppers
1 onion
1 6-oz can black olives
8-oz mozzarella cheese

1. How many batches of punch does Amita need? _____

2. How many batches of cupcakes does Amita need? _____

3. How many pizzas does Amita need? _____

Here are the prices of the ingredients at the grocery store. Fill in the chart with what Amita needs for her party.

Ingredients	Unit Cost	Number Needed	Total Cost
1 (2-liter bottle) lemon-lime soda	$0.89		
1 quart orange sherbet	$1.29		
1 quart vanilla ice cream	$2.99		
1 (32-oz) can tomato sauce	$1.09		
1 bag pizza dough	$1.19		
1 head of broccoli	$0.79		
1 container mushrooms	$2.29		
1 bell pepper	$0.69		
1 onion	$0.52		
1 (6-oz) can black olives	$1.59		
1 package cupcake mix	$2.99		
32 oz mozzarella cheese	$4.99		

4. Does Amita have enough money? _____

5. How much money does Amita have left over? _____

6. How much money can Amita save by using vegetables from her mother's garden instead of buying them? _____

Sudoku

Fill in the grid so that every row, column, and 3 × 3 box contains the numbers 1 through 9.

	3	2			1		9	7
6			7	5			2	4
	5		4		2	8	1	6
	1	6		9	7	2		
			8	2	4			
		4	5	1		9	7	
2	7	3	1		8		5	
1	4			6	5			2
9	6		2			4	8	

Fill in the grid so that every row, column, and 3 × 3 box contains the letters A through I.

		I	B		C	G		F
	C	B	A		G	H		E
F		A			H		B	D
		D	F	H		I		C
			E	C	I			
C		E		G	B	A		
B	E		G			F		I
A		G	H		F	E	C	
I		H	C		E	D		

Decimal Sudoku

Fill in the grid so that every row, column, and 3 × 3 box contains the numbers 0.1 to 0.9.

	0.6			0.2	0.8	0.5		0.4
0.2		0.4		0.6				0.9
			0.9		0.1		0.2	0.8
0.1		0.6		0.8			0.9	
0.4	0.7		0.1					0.6
	0.3		0.6					
0.8				0.1	0.6	0.9		0.5
0.6		0.7			0.4	0.1	0.8	0.3
0.3			0.8	0.7	0.9	0.4	0.6	0.2

Shape Sudoku

Fill in the grid so every row, column, and 3 × 2 box has one of each of the shapes in the box.

Mixed Math Squares

Use the numbers 1–9 to fill in the missing numbers in the math squares. Use each number once. Each row and each column is a math equation.

Puzzle 1

	−		−		**−5**
−	■	−	■	×	
	+		×		**10**
+	■	−	■	−	
	/		−		**−5**

Column answers: **6**   **−1**   **−3**

Puzzle 2

	×		−		**−1**
/	■	−	■	−	
	−		+		**4**
−	■	/	■	−	
	×		/		**2**

Column answers: **1**   **−1**   **−4**

Lattice Multiplication

The mathematician Fibonacci introduced lattice multiplication to Europe in the 1200s. Read the explanation in the box, then use lattice multiplication to find the products below.

Step 1: Write the numbers you are multiplying along the top and side of the grid.
Step 2: Multiply each top digit by each side digit.
Step 3: Beginning at the lower right, add diagonally to find your answer. Note: when adding, you may have to carry double-digit sums to the next diagonal.
Step 4: Read the numbers along the left and bottom to see the product.

Example: 427 × 73

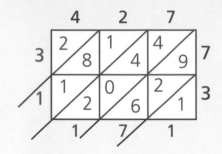

The product is 31,171.

1. 369 × 47

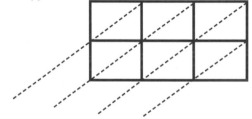

The product is _____.

2. 528 × 65

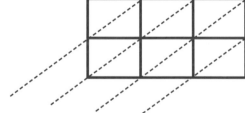

The product is _____.

3. 471 × 240

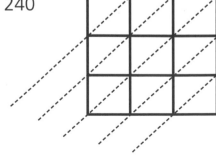

The product is _____.

4. 857 × 913

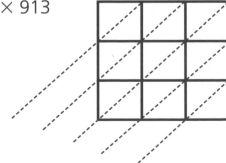

The product is _____.

Exciting Elevens

Find the patterns, then answer the questions below.

11 × 1 = _____	12 × 1 = _____	13 × 1 = _____
11 × 11 = _____	12 × 11 = _____	13 × 11 = _____
11 × 111 = _____	12 × 111 = _____	13 × 111 = _____

Now see how quickly you can find the answers to these multiplication problems using the same pattern.

1. 14 × 11 = _____

2. 15 × 111 = _____

3. 16 × 1,111 = _____

4. 17 × 11,111 = _____

5. 18 × 111,111 = _____

6. 11 × 1,111 = _____

7. 12 × 11,111 = _____

8. 13 × 111,111 = _____

Batter Up!

Enfield's minor-league baseball team has just finished its season. Coach Mimson needs to know everyone's batting average to give out the trophies. To find the batting average, divide the number of hits by the number of at-bats. The best you can have is 1.00. So, unless the batter got a hit every time he was at bat, the average will be a decimal. Fill in the charts below to help out the coach. Round to the nearest thousandth.

Player	Hits	At-Bats	Batting Average
Aaron	13	32	
Bert	18	27	
Charles	9	29	
Darnell	11	33	
Eli	7	24	
Francis	15	31	
Gary	19	26	
Hassid	23	35	
Ian	8	21	

Place	Player
1st	
2nd	
3rd	
4th	
5th	
6th	
7th	
8th	
9th	

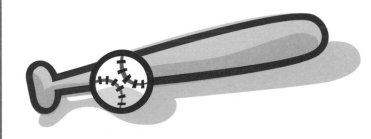

Comparing Fractions and Decimals

Label each fraction, decimal, or mixed number on the number line.
Then write <, >, or =.

1. $\dfrac{3}{4}$ _____ 0.8

2. $1\dfrac{2}{4}$ _____ 1.5

3. 0.5 _____ $\dfrac{5}{8}$

4. $4\dfrac{1}{4}$ _____ 4.2

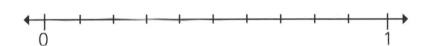

5. $5\dfrac{1}{2}$ _____ $\dfrac{11}{2}$

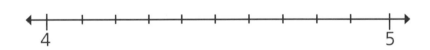

6. $\dfrac{3}{8}$ _____ 0.3

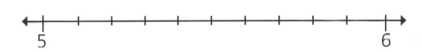

7. $\dfrac{27}{4}$ _____ 6.75

8. $\dfrac{2}{3}$ _____ 0.9

Challenging Circle Graphs

For each circle graph below, find out how many people each slice represents. Then use the legend to complete the circle graphs.

1.

Favorite Fruit	
Apple	4
Banana	2
Orange	2
Strawberry	8

Apple   Banana   Orange   Strawberry

Each slice stands for _____ people.

2.

Favorite Season	
Winter	3
Spring	6
Summer	12
Fall	3

Winter   Spring   Summer   Fall

Each slice stands for _____ people.

3.

Favorite Subject	
Math	10
English	15
Science	10
Social Studies	5

■ Math   ■ English   ■ Science   ■ Social Studies

Each slice stands for _____ people.

4.

New Team Name	
Wildcats	12
Chargers	16
Science	0
Wombats	4

■ Wildcats   ■ Chargers   ■ Wombats   ■ Tigers

Each slice stands for _____ people.

Find the pattern and fill in the missing squares.

0.25	0.25	0.25	0.25
0.25	0.75	1.25	1.75
0.25	1.25	3.25	6.25
0.25			

Now make your own square using the same pattern and leave one blank for a friend to solve.

Number Lines

Beatrice is making number lines for a class project. Help her put the correct decimal at each point.

1.

A   B   C   D   E   F   G   H   I   J   K

0   1

2.

A   B   C   D   E

0   1

3.

A   B   C

0   1

4.

A   B   C   D   E   F

0   1

Rambling Rick

Rick has written some word problems for you to solve. Rick likes to ramble on, and he included information that you don't need to solve each problem. Rewrite each word problem without the unnecessary information. Then solve the problems.

1. It was Thursday. Phillip went to the store. The store was the supermarket. He spent $15.42. The last time he went to the store he spent only $9.08. But this time he was hungry so he bought lots of snacks. Phillip likes cookies. He gave the cashier $20, but he had $30 in his pocket. What was his change?

   _____

   _____

   _____

   _____

2. I have a friend named Elaine. Elaine likes to walk. She walks whenever she can. She walked 3.21 miles on Monday, 4.73 miles on Tuesday, and 6.05 miles on Wednesday. On Thursday she was tired. Friday she bought new sneakers at the mall, but she drove there. The mall is 9.5 miles from her house. Elaine's house is 5.95 miles from my house. How many miles did she walk altogether?

   _____

   _____

   _____

   _____

3. Nathaniel gets up at 8:05 AM for school. He is in the fourth grade. He eats breakfast and brushes his teeth. He has eggs for breakfast. It takes him 34 minutes to get ready for school. He leaves when he is ready. School starts at 9:00. It gets out at 2:30. Then Nathaniel has baseball practice. What time does Nathaniel leave for school?

   _____

   _____

4. At a bake sale, Ellie sold 4 dozen cookies before lunch. She also sold 2 dozen muffins. After lunch, she sold another 5 dozen cookies. The cookies were chocolate chip. The muffins were blueberry. When it was time to leave, she had $1\frac{1}{2}$ dozen cookies left. The cookies were $0.25 each. How many cookies did Ellie have at the start of the bake sale?

_____

_____

_____

_____

5. Louis, Harold, and Damian are friends. They like to collect sports cards. Louis has 2,523 baseball cards and 962 hockey cards. James has 4,278 stamps. Harold has 4,862 baseball cards and 6,956 basketball cards. Damian has 3,657 football cards and 3,957 baseball cards. How many baseball cards do Louis, Harold, and Damian have altogether?

_____

_____

_____

_____

Valuable Variables

Use the equations below to determine the value of each shape. No number is represented by more than one shape and no shape is equal to 0. The value of each shape is constant for all problems and can only be 1-9.

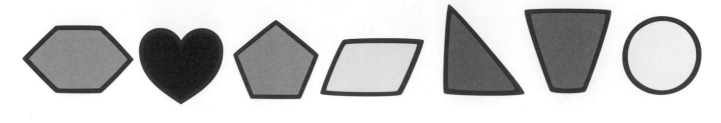

_____   _____   _____   _____   _____   _____   _____

1. ⬡ + ⬡ = 10

2. ♥ − ⬡ = 3

3. ⬠ − ▱ = 4 and ⬠ + ▱ = 10

4. ◺ − 1 = ♥

5. ◺ − ⬡ = ⬯

6. ⬯ + ◯ = 6

184

Two Variables

Equations can have two variables. When you solve an equation with two variables, you have to find all the solutions. Find all the solutions to the equations below. Remember that each variable has a different value.

1. ▲ + ■ = 6

▲	■
6	
5	
4	
2	
1	
0	

2. ● × ■ = 24

●	■

3. $e + q = 10$

e	q

4. $h \times i = 60$

h	i

Answer Key

Page 4
Answers will vary, but here is an example of a completed map:

Page 5
1. Action; C
2. Mystery; D
3. Mystery; A
4. Sci-Fi; B
5. Action; D
6. Action and Sci-Fi; A

Page 6

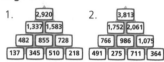

1.
| 2,920 |
1,337	1,583
482	855	728
137	345	510	218

2.
| 3,813 |
1,752	2,061
766	986	1,075
491	275	711	364

3.
| 2,884 |
1,733	1,151
1,185	548	603
833	352	196	407

4.
| 7,385 |
3,728	3,657
1,789	1,939	1,718
844	945	994	724
284	560	385	609	115

Page 7
1. 3.79
2. 7.59
3. 9.41
4. 6.38
5. 11.33
6. 7.89
7. 7.38
8. 9.16
9. 15.26
10. Answers will vary.

Page 8
Possible answers include:

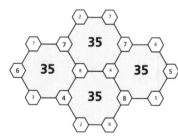

Page 9
The mystery number is 49.

Page 10
Puzzle answer: We've got problems!

Page 11
1. 10 years old, public school, 200 students
2. 5 years old, private school, 100 students
3. The school drawn should have

4 flags, a clock, 5 windows
4. The school drawn should have 3 flags, no clock, 6 windows

Pages 12–13
1. Dog: 10, Cat: 8, Horse: 5, Frog: 4, Bird: 8, Snake: 7
2. 42
3. dog
4. frog
5. Dog: $\frac{10}{42}$, Cat: $\frac{8}{42}$, Horse: $\frac{5}{42}$, Frog: $\frac{4}{42}$, Bird: $\frac{8}{42}$, Snake: $\frac{7}{42}$
6. Answers will vary.
7. Answers will vary.
8. Answers will vary.

Page 14
1. 23, 24, 30, 31
2. 14, 15, 21, 22
3. 1, 2, 8, 9
4. 10, 11, 17, 18
5. 19, 20, 26, 27
6. 6, 7, 13, 14

Page 15
1. 7, 14, 15
2. 22, 29, 30
3. 20, 27, 28
4. 10, 17, 18
5. 3, 10, 11
6. 16, 23, 24

Page 16
Message: I am getting a puppy!

Page 17
1.
2.
3.
4.
5. 43,036
6. 762,428
7. 258,103
8. 2,213,205

Page 18
1. 12, 4, 2
2. 4, 3, 2
3. 6, 8, 3, 2, 2, 2
4. The bottom row of each factor tree should contain 2, 2, 3, and 5.

Page 19

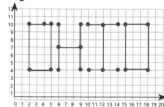

Riddle answer: Ohio

Page 20
Nancy is thinking of the number 52.

Page 21

Class	Boxes Sold
Room 401	
Room 402	
Room 403	
Room 404	
Room 405	
Room 406	

1. Room 406
2. Room 404
3. 16 boxes
4. $33\frac{3}{4}$ cookies

Page 22

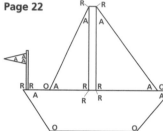

Page 23
1. 6 − 3 + 2 = 5
2. 80 + 37 − 51 = 66
3. 65 − 3 − 4 = 58
4. 77 + 4 − 3 = 78
5. 60 + 6 + 38 − 9 = 95
6. 76 + 19 + 46 + 1 = 142
7. 97 − 11 + 49 − 19 = 116
8. 8 − 37 + 33 = 4

Page 24
Row 1: 179,602; 215,638; 287,926
Row 2: 443,498; 456,760; 615,726; 388,820
Row 3: 720,656; 856,848; 716,620
Row 4: 468,153; 830,841; 552,610; 996,726
Row 5: 578,338; 526,603; 832,716
Row 6: 990,940; 548,877; 789,702; 944,877
Row 7: 961,479; 811,976; 901,863
Row 8: 943,564; 658,462; 875,720; 986,885
Row 9: 640,547; 722,206; 960,742

Page 25
1. 1080°
2. 540°
3. 720°
4. 900°
5. 360°
6. 1440°

Pages 26–27
1. triangle, $\frac{1}{2}$
2. $\frac{1}{8}$
3. $\frac{1}{16}$
4. square, $\frac{1}{2}$
5. $\frac{1}{4}$
6. 40 triangles, 10 squares
7. obtuse
8. acute
9. right
10. parallel
11. perpendicular
12. Possible answers include: HLG, MKF, AIB BJC

Page 28
1. 3 units
2. 4 units
3. 6 units
4. 4 units
5. 8 units
6. 23 units

Page 29
1. 4 weeks 3 days
2. 3 years 10 months
3. 2 days 9 hours
4. 3 minutes 2 seconds
5. 42 months
6. 323 minutes
7. 60 days
8. 74 hours

Page 30
1. parallelograms
2. trapezoids
3. rhombuses
4. quadrilaterals

Page 31
1. 17
2. 34
3. 61
4. 1,094
5. 1,745
6. XXXVIII
7. CCCLXIV
8. MMMCDLXXII
9. MMCMLXXXVII
10. MCCXCIII

Page 32
1. 0.343434…
2. 0.444…
3. 0.867867867…
4. 0.009009009…
5. 0.787878…
6. 0.222…
7. 0.050505…
8. 0.998998998…
9. 0.062062062…
10. 0.070070070…

Page 33
1. 10 AM, 10 AM, 9 AM, 9 AM, 8 AM, 10 AM, 5 AM, 5 AM, 7 AM, 10 AM, 7 AM, 7 AM, 8 AM, 10 AM
2. 1:00 PM
3. 7:00 PM
4. Answers will vary.

Pages 34–35
1. trapezoid
2. parallelogram
3. triangle
4. 3 units
5. 5 units
6. Possible answers include: home to school to Min's house to home, school to the library to Min's house to school, home to school to the store to home
7. parallel
8. perpendicular
9. obtuse
10. acute
11. right
12. (4, 6)

Page 36
1. yes   2. no   3. no
4. yes   5. yes   6. no
7. no   8. no

Page 37
1. yes   2. yes   3. no
4. no   5. yes   6. no
7. yes   8. no

Page 38
1. yes   2. no   3. yes
4. yes   5. yes   6. no
7. no   8. no

Page 39
1. no   2. yes   3. no
4. no   5. yes   6. yes
7. yes   8. no

Page 40
1. no   2. yes   3. no
4. yes   5. yes   6. no
7. no   8. yes

Page 41

A	1
B	3
C	7
D	9
E	13
F	15
G	19
H	21
I	25
J	27
K	31
L	33
M	37
N	39
O	43
P	45
Q	49
R	51
S	55
T	57
U	61
V	63
W	67
X	69
Y	73
Z	75

Secret Code: DO YOU WANT TO COME OVER AFTER SCHOOL?

Page 42
1. 2 apples
2. 3 problems
3. 4 books
4. 2 people
5. 7 pretzels
6. 4 cups

Page 43
1. 4,096; multiply by 8
2. 7; divide by 7
3. 1,771,561; multiply by 11
4. 279,936; multiply by 6
5. 40; divide by 2
6. 15,625; multiply by 5
7. 100; divide by 10
8. 65,536; multiply by 4
9. 4,826,809; multiply by 13
10. 81; divide by 9

Page 44
1. $\frac{28}{100}$; shade 28 boxes
2. $\frac{74}{100}$; shade 74 boxes
3. $\frac{62}{100}$; shade 62 boxes
4. $\frac{56}{100}$; shade 56 boxes

Page 45
1. 31 stuffed animals
2. $1.40
3. $2.75
4. 22 cards
5. 36 years old
6. $6.00

Page 46

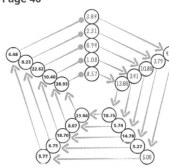

Page 47
1. $3\frac{1}{2}$
2. $3\frac{2}{3}$
3. $4\frac{2}{4}$
4. $5\frac{3}{5}$
5. $5\frac{5}{6}$
6. $5\frac{3}{8}$
7. 6
8. $5\frac{4}{12}$

Page 48
1. 7.90   2. 7.58
3. 8.30   4. 8.53
5. 8.65   6. 8.13

Place	Gymnast
Gold	Etienne
Silver	Sven
Bronze	Zoe
4th	Carlos
5th	Kelly
6th	Juan

Page 49
13; 21; 34; 55; 89; 144; 233; 377; 610; 987; 1,597; 2,584; 4,181; 6,765; 10,946; 17,711; 28,657; 46,368; 75,025; 121,393; 196,418; 317,811; 514,229
Answers to the question will vary.

Page 50
1. Maple and Winter; Spring, Birch, and Winter; or Maple, Fall Birch, and Winter
2. Maple and Winter
3. Summer, Winter, or Spring
4. Birch
5. Spring and Pine

Page 51
1. 4   2. 2
3. 1   4. 3
5. 7   6. 8
7. 0   8. 5
Riddle answer: YOUR NAME!

Page 52
1. $7\frac{3}{6}$
2. $46\frac{3}{7}$
3. $18\frac{1}{4}$
4. $65\frac{5}{8}$
5. $288\frac{1}{9}$
6. $1,603\frac{2}{5}$
7. $22,436\frac{1}{3}$
8. $24,947\frac{5}{7}$

Page 53
6,579,834; six million, five hundred seventy-nine thousand, eight hundred thirty-four

Page 54
283,291.67

Page 55

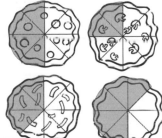

1. 58
2. 36.83
3. 37.5
4. 31.63

Page 56
1. 5 h 35 min
2. 25 min
3. 10 h 45 min
4. 1 h 22 min
5. 10 h 8 min
6. 27 min
7. 11 h
8. 2 h 45 min

Page 57
1.   2.
3.   4.
5.   6.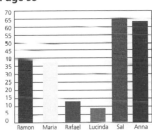

Page 58

Page 59

1. green
2. yellow
3. red
4. blue

Page 60

Least to most: Paula, Larry, Mitch, Helene

Page 61
2. $\frac{5}{13}$
3. $\frac{5}{6}$
4. $\frac{7}{13}$
5. $\frac{1}{6}$
6. $\frac{2}{6}$
7. $\frac{1}{5}$
8. $\frac{8}{13}$
9. $\frac{2}{8}$
10. $\frac{6}{19}$

Pages 62–63

TRANSACTIONS	DEBIT (−) (WITHDRAWAL)	CREDIT(+) (DEPOSIT)	BALANCE
Deposit		347 23	$347 23
Video game withdrawal	−$50 75		$296 48
Money earned mowing lawns		25 50	$321 98
Gift for mom	−$22 45		$299 53
Money lent to sister	−$10 20		$289 33
Allowance		5 00	$294 33
Fish tank supplies	−$32 75		$261 58
CD	−$19 99		$241 59
DVD	$18 33		$223 26
Interest earned		90	$224 16

You have $224.16 left.

Page 64
1. 32 in.²
2. 16 ft²
3. 124 mi²
4. 320 m²
5. 96 cm²
6. 277 km²

Page 65

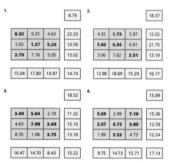

Page 66
1. 63,518
2. 394,295
3. 790
4. 832,542
5. 37,459
6.

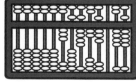

Page 67
1. 0.88
2. 2.53
3. 31.07
4. 631.87
5. 31,820.42
6.

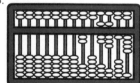

Page 68

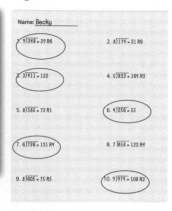

Name: Becky
1. 9)348 = 39 R6
2. 8)174 = 21 R6
3. 3)411 = 132
4. 5)822 = 164 R2
5. 8)585 = 73 R1
6. 4)256 = 55
7. 6)736 = 121 R4
8. 7)858 = 122 R4
9. 8)605 = 75 R5
10. 9)974 = 108 R3

Page 69

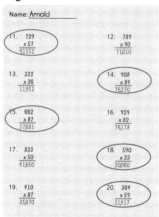

Name: Arnold
11. 729 × 57 = 41,552
12. 789 × 90 = 71,010
13. 332 × 36 = 11,952
14. 908 × 84 = 76,270
15. 662 × 87 = 57,681
16. 929 × 82 = 76,178
17. 833 × 50 = 41,650
18. 590 × 33 = 20,060
19. 410 × 87 = 35,870
20. 364 × 59 = 21,417

Page 70

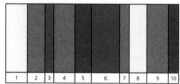

Page 71
1. 6, 1, 7, 6
2. 6, 7, 9, 6, 5
3. 1, 6, 4, 1, 1
4. 2, 8, 1, 6
5. 9, 4, 0, 3, 1, 8
6. 8, 2, 1, 6, 5
7. 7, 0, 6, 8, 5
8. 2, 9, 2, 0, 6
9. 7, 3, 6, 8

Page 72
1. $\frac{9}{2} = 4\frac{1}{2}$
2. $\frac{37}{6} = 6\frac{1}{6}$
3. $\frac{14}{9} = 1\frac{5}{9}$
4. $\frac{20}{3} = 6\frac{2}{3}$
5. $\frac{32}{9} = 3\frac{5}{9}$
6. $\frac{13}{3} = 4\frac{1}{3}$
7. $\frac{13}{6} = 2\frac{1}{6}$

Page 73
1. Omar is the winner.
2. 99,544; 413; 73,794; 30,277

Page 74
1. 8 × 49 ÷ 7 = 56
2. 85 ÷ 5 × 2 = 34
3. 56 ÷ 4 × 39 = 546
4. 84 × 50 ÷ 5 = 840
5. 36 ÷ 2 × 3 ÷ 18 = 3
6. 15 × 4 ÷ 3 × 2 = 40
7. 2 × 5 ÷ 10 × 2 = 2
8. 42 ÷ 6 × 5 × 2 = 70

Page 75
Answers will vary.

Pages 76–77
1. (24, 6)
2. (6, 18)
3. (7, 16)
4. (14, 41)
5. #4
6. #2
7. #1
8. #3
9. #2
10. #3
11. #1
12. #4
13. (1, 1) (2, 5) (3, 9)
14. (1, 15) (2, 20) (3, 25)
15. (1, 3) (2,10) (3,17)
16. (1,13) (2, 26) (3, 39)

Page 78

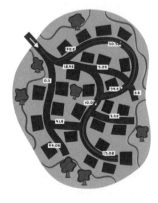

Page 79

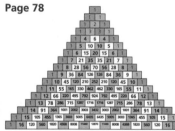

Page 80
1. LXIX
2. CXLIII
3. CLX
4. DCCLXV
5. MMMCCLXXXIII
6. MCMLII
7. DCCXXXVIII
8. MMMMMCCCLXXI

Page 81

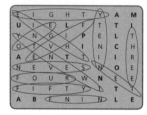

Page 82
The completed drawing should show books stacked in a pyramid with rows of: 1, 2, 3, 4, 5, 6, 7, 8, 9, 10, 11, and 12.

Page 83
1. Color in 4 bars.
2. Color in 5 bars.
3. Color in 1 bar.
4. Color in 3 bars.
5. Color in 6 bars.

Pages 84–85

1. twenty
2. eight
3. five
4. ten
5. nine
6. eighty
7. one
8. seven
9. fifty
10. four
11. ninety
12. three
Riddle answer: A MULTIPLICATION TABLE

Page 86
1. 1.5-lb bag of rice
2. 16-oz box of cereal
3. half gallon of milk
4. 3 shirts for $3.00 each
5. bag of 14 apples
6. box of pencils for $1.29
7. package of 150 sheets
8. loaf of bread for $0.99
9. box of 10 cans of soup
10. 2-lb bag of flour

Page 87

Puppy T-shirt	ⲦⲎⲦ ⲦⲎⲦ ⲦⲎⲦ Ⲓ
Sandy's Store Logo T-shirt	ⲦⲎⲦ ⲦⲎⲦ ⲦⲎⲦ ⲦⲎⲦ ⅠⅠⅠⅠ
Sun T-shirt	ⲦⲎⲦ ⅠⅠⅠ

Page 88
1. 1,164,925
2. 1,713,550
3. 3,817,375
4. 9,131,225
5. 16,243,100
6. 112,809,125
7. 213,658,200
8. 643,746,625

Page 89
1. 57,250
2. 114,250
3. 182,000
4. 684,875
5. 5,320,875
6. 10,570,375
7. 56,408,500
8. 120,664,625

Page 90

$y = 3x + 2$

x	y
0	2
1	5
2	8
3	11
4	14
5	17
6	20

$y = -x + 9$

x	y
0	9
1	8
2	7
3	6
4	5
5	4
6	3

$y = 3x - 6$

x	y
0	−6
1	−3
2	0
3	3
4	6
5	9
6	12

$y = -4x + 9$

x	y
0	9
1	5
2	1
3	−3
4	−7
5	−11
6	−15

Page 91
1. 37 boys, 43 girls
2. 2 dimes, 1 nickel
3. 6 peanut butter, 12 chocolate chip, 18 sugar
4. 30 chocolate, 15 vanilla, 10 strawberry, 5 lemon
5. 10 red, 14 blue, 18 yellow
6. 1,575

Page 92
1. $\frac{2}{5}$ 2. $\frac{1}{4}$
3. $\frac{3}{8}$ 4. $\frac{6}{10}$

Page 93

3	5	8	4	3	8
6	9	2	8	1	0
3	8	7	2	2	1
9	8	5	4	0	6
5	3	1	4	7	6
9	3	2	0	5	1

1. 932,051
2. 827,512
3. 801,661
4. 692,810
5. 358,438
6. 531,476
7. 482,440
8. 312,075
9. 985,406
10. 363,959
11. 598,833
12. 387,221

Page 94
Answers will vary. Here is an example of a picture that is colored correctly.

Page 95
1.

2.

3.

4.

Page 96
Congruent figures include:
1 and 7, 2 and 5, 6 and 8
Shapes drawn at the bottom of the page should be the same size and shape as 3 and 4.

Page 97

Colors	Tally	Number
Blue	ⲦⲎⲦ ⲦⲎⲦ ⅠⅠ	12
Red	ⲦⲎⲦ Ⅰ	6
Yellow	ⅠⅠⅠⅠ	4
Green	ⲦⲎⲦ ⲦⲎⲦ ⲦⲎⲦ ⅠⅠⅠ	18

Page 98

1. $\frac{1}{2}$

2. $\frac{2}{4}$, $\frac{3}{6}$, $\frac{4}{8}$, $\frac{5}{10}$

3. , $\frac{3}{6}$

4. $\frac{1}{4}$

5. $\frac{2}{8}$, $\frac{3}{12}$, $\frac{4}{16}$, $\frac{5}{20}$

Page 99
Row 1: 10,626; 7,854; 5,542
Row 2: 4,117; 18,018; 11,186; 16,626
Row 3: 6,981; 25,662; 33,558
Row 4: 13,067; 11,271; 8,554; 8,313
Row 5: 21,097; 3,757; 2,119
Row 6: 43,289; 7,514; 50,765; 2,934
Row 7: 15,418; 101,530; 70,290

Page 100
Answers will vary.

Page 101
1. the area that 1 gallon of paint covers
2. the number of students in your class
3. how many miles away your friend lives
4. how many siblings there are
5. how much each dog weighs
6. how many yards of ribbon are on a spool

Page 102
1. 29 marbles
2. 35 dollars
3. 7 PM
4. 10 kittens
5. 12 feet

Page 103
1. 0°F
2. 100 − (−18) = 118°
3. 30 − 40 = −10°F
4. −6 + 12 = 6°F
5. 20 − (−18) = 38°
6. swimming
7. −10°C

Pages 104–105
1. cube
2. triangular pyramid
3. square pyramid
4. octahedron
5. rectangular prism
6. cone
7. cylinder
8. triangular prism

Page 106
 = $0.49

 = $0.79

 = $0.29

Page 107
1.

300	6	**50**
10	**1**	10
30	6	5

2.

450	**5**	90
3	1	3
150	**5**	30

3.

672	6	**112**
8	2	4
84	3	28

4.

324	**9**	36
12	3	**4**
27	**3**	9

Page 108
1. 124,578
2. 875,421
3. 872,541
4. 124,587
5. 875,412
6. 142,578
7. 125,874
8. 478,512

Page 109
1. goes   2. hose
3. soil   4. shoe
5. sigh   6. loose
7. hills   8. shells

Page 110
1.

2.

3.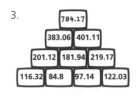

4.

Page 111
1. 11:00   2. 10:00
3. 10:30   4. 12:00
5. 11:30   6. 10:45
7. 10:15   8. 12:15

Child	Time	Child	Time
Billy	10:00	Abby	11:00
Gert	10:15	Ellie	11:30
Carly	10:30	Devon	12:00
Freddy	10:45	Henry	12:15

Page 112
Alan's birthday is October 17 (Friday). Natalie's birthday is October 10 (Friday). Rita's birthday is October 26 (Sunday). Seth's birthday is October 2 (Thursday).

Page 113
1. $\frac{3}{4} = 0.75$
2. $\frac{4}{5} = 0.80$
3. $\frac{4}{9} = 0.444$,
   $\frac{5}{9} = 0.555$,
   $\frac{6}{9} = 0.666$,
   $\frac{7}{9} = 0.777$,
   $\frac{8}{9} = 0.888$
4. $\frac{3}{10} = 0.30$,
   $\frac{4}{10} = 0.40$,
   $\frac{5}{10} = 0.50$,
   $\frac{6}{10} = 0.60$,
   $\frac{7}{10} = 0.70$,
   $\frac{8}{10} = 0.80$,
   $\frac{9}{10} = 0.90$
5. $\frac{4}{11} = 0.3636$,
   $\frac{5}{11} = 0.4545$,
   $\frac{6}{11} = 0.5454$,
   $\frac{7}{11} = 0.6363$,
   $\frac{8}{11} = 0.7272$,
   $\frac{9}{11} = 0.8181$,
   $\frac{10}{11} = 0.9090$,

Page 114
These numbers are circled:
1. 273   2. 300
3. 81   4. 318
5. 369   6. 612
7. 123   8. 300
9. 999   10. 333
They are all multiples of 3.

Page 115
1. addition
2. subtraction
3. multiplication
4. division
5. 5,000
6. 38

Page 116
1. 27,924
2. 50,180
3. 81,588
4. 127,608
5. 2,739,256
6. 3,372,356
7. 12,300,496
8. 16,258,268

Page 117
1. $\frac{3}{12}$ 2. $\frac{8}{16}$
3. $\frac{6}{9}$ 4. $\frac{12}{16}$
5. $\frac{5}{15}$ 6. $\frac{10}{20}$
7. $\frac{2}{8}$ 8. $\frac{4}{6}$

Page 118
1. 8.75
2. 10
3. 9.5
4. 9.75
5. 12
6. 8.25
7. 9.75
8. 9
9. 10.5
10. 10.25
11. 8.5
12. 9

Page 119

	Hexagon	Octagon	Rectangle	Triangle	Square
Baseball	X	X	O	X	X
Basketball	O	X	X	X	X
Football	X	X	X	X	O
Hockey	X	X	X	O	X
Soccer	X	O	X	X	X

Pages 120–121
1. 2, 3, 5, 7, 11, 13, 17, 19, 23, 29, 31, 37, 41, 43, 47, 53, 59, 61, 67, 71, 73, 79, 83, 89, 97
2. If a number is divisible by a number other than 1 or itself, it is not prime.

Page 122
101, 103, 107, 109, 113, 127, 131, 137, 139, 149, 151, 157, 163, 167, 173, 179, 181, 191, 193, 197, 199

Page 123
1. 5 and 7
2. 11 and 5
3. 13 and 7, 17 and 3
4. 19 and 5, 17 and 7, 13 and 11
5. 17 and 17, 23 and 11, 29 and 5, 31 and 3
6. 23 and 23, 29 and 17, 41 and 5, 43 and 3
7. 29 and 29, 47 and 11, 41 and 17, 53 and 5
8. 53 and 7, 47 and 13, 43 and 17, 41 and 19, 37 and 23, 31 and 29
9. 53, 17, and 2; 47, 23, and 2; 41, 29, and 2; 67, 2, and 3; 59, 11, and 2
10. 73, 5, and 2; 71, 7, and 2; 67, 11, and 2; 61, 17, and 2; 59, 19, and 2; 47, 31, and 2; 41, 37, and 2

Page 124

	Lap 1	Lap 2	Total Time	Place
Clyde	29.39 seconds	29.18 seconds	58.57 seconds	3rd
Howie	30.39 seconds	30.51 seconds	60.9 seconds	4th
Laura	28.220 seconds	28.187 seconds	56.407 seconds	1st
Maddy	28.75 seconds	29.72 seconds	58.47 seconds	2nd

Page 125

	307	317	319	340	350
Alexis	X	X	X	O	X
David	X	X	O	X	X
Katherine	O	X	X	X	X
Mackenzie	X	O	X	X	X
Nate	X	X	X	X	O

Page 126
1. 2   2. 11
3. 24   4. 47
5. 8   6. 55
7. 39   8. 6

Page 127
1. Alison worked 38 hours at $10 per hour for a total of $380.
2. Jo worked 37 hours at $15 per hour for a total of $555.
3. Rebecca worked 40 hours at $9 per hour for a total of $360.
4. Rodney worked 47 hours at $11 per hour for a total of $517.

Page 128
1. $0 = 99 - 99$ or $0 = (9 \div 9) - (9 \div 9)$
2. $2 = (99 \div 9) - 9$ or $2 = (9 \div 9) + (9 \div 9)$
3. $20 = (99 \div 9) + 9$
4. $81 = 9 \times 9 \div 9 \times 9$ or $81 = (9 \times 9) \times (9 \div 9)$
5. $98 = 99 - (9 \div 9)$
6. $99 = 99 \times (9 \div 9)$
7. $100 = 99 + (9 \div 9)$
8. $180 = (9 \times 9) + 99$

Page 129
1. 5
2. 24
3. 29
4. 16
5. 12
6. 30
7. 71
8. 183
9. 19
10. 184

Page 130
Everyone has the 11th free.

Page 131
1. 435,600
2. 352,917
3. 924,031
4. 518,267
5. 519,046
6. 691,754
7. 159,814
8. 742,207
9. 819,011
10. 432,498

Page 132

Teacher	Magazines Recycled	Cans Recycled
Mrs. Brown's	24	129
Mrs. Finch's	29	107
Mr. Bartoli's	23	112
Miss Johnson's	20	139

Page 133

$\div 9 = \triangle$ R $\bullet$

	$\triangle$	$\bullet$
134	14	8
243	27	0
598	66	4
997	110	7
1,837	204	1
6,358	706	4

$\div 7 = \triangle$ R $\bullet$

	$\triangle$	$\bullet$
359	51	2
638	91	1
796	113	5
864	123	3
1,638	234	0
9,374	1,339	1

Page 134
1.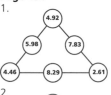

2.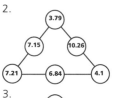

3.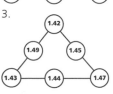

Page 135
14,406 pieces of cheese
$7 \times 7 \times 7 \times 7 \times 3 \times 2 = 14,406$

Page 136

Child	Place	Project
Nona	1st	ant farm
Keenan	2nd	volcano
Tracy	3rd	sea monkeys

Page 137
45 handshakes
Anderson and Bartleby; Anderson and Coleman; Anderson and D'Agostino; Anderson and Engers; Anderson and Finch; Anderson and Garero; Anderson and Henderson; Anderson and Ichiro; Anderson and Jiminez; Bartleby and Coleman; Bartleby and D'Agostino; Bartleby and Engers; Bartleby and Finch; Bartleby and Garero; Bartleby and Henderson; Bartleby and Ichiro; Bartleby and Jiminez; Coleman and D'Agostino; Coleman and Engers; Coleman and Finch; Coleman and Garero; Coleman and Henderson; Coleman and Ichiro; Coleman and Jiminez; D'Agostino and Engers; D'Agostino and Finch; D'Agostino and Garero; D'Agostino and Henderson; D'Agostino and Ichiro; D'Agostino and Jiminez; Engers and Finch; Engers and Garero; Engers and Henderson; Engers and Ichiro; Engers and Jiminez; Finch and Garero; Finch and Henderson; Finch and Ichiro; Finch and Jiminez; Garero and Henderson; Garero and Ichiro; Garero and Jiminez; Henderson and Ichiro; Henderson and Jiminez; Ichiro and Jiminez

Page 138
1. $12.57   2. $7.26
3. $4.83   4. $2.99
5. $27.65   6. $2.35

Page 139
A googol has one hundred zeroes.

Page 140
1. $(7 + 8) \times 9 + 4 = 139$
2. $6 \times 7 + 26 - (19 + 4) = 45$
3. $(31 + 8) \times 2 = 78$
4. $(3 + 4) \times 7 + 309 - 3 \times 3 = 349$
5. $17 \times (10 + 9) + 8 \div 4 = 325$
6. $(12,942 - 42) \div 5 = 2,580$
7. $2,646 \div 14 \times (7 - 5) = 378$
8. $429 \times 3 - 168 \div (4 - 2) = 1,203$
9. $(80 + 19 + 21) \div 10 = 12$
10. $(3,729 + 1,271) \div (2 + 2 + 1) = 1,000$

Page 141
1. 30
2. 35
3. 40
4. 39

5. 33
6. 30
7. 38
8. 34
9. 34
10. 36

Page 142
1. 2.56, 2.58, 2.59, 2.61, 2.64
2. 8.5, 8.6, 8.9, 9.1, 9.2, 9.4
3. 1.82, 1.84
4. 21.5, 21.6, 21.8, 21.9, 22.1, 22.4
5. 5.94
6. 6.8, 6.9
7. 58.6, 58.9, 59.1, 59.2, 59.4
8. 8.45
9. 1.5, 1.6, 1.8, 1.9, 2.1, 2.4
10. 1.2

Page 143
1. A and B, C and E
2. A, C, D, and E; or B, C, E, and F
3. C, D, E, and G; A, B, C, D, E, and F; or C, E, F, and G
4. A, B, C, E, and F
5. quadrilateral
6.

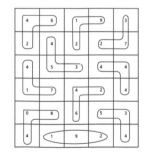

Page 144
1. $\frac{4}{10}$, 0.4
2. $\frac{2}{10}$, 0.2
3. $\frac{1}{10}$, 0.1
4. $\frac{3}{10}$, 0.3
5. $\frac{7}{100}$, 0.07
6. $\frac{22}{100}$, 0.22
7. $\frac{39}{100}$, 0.39
8. $\frac{32}{100}$, 0.32

Page 145

Page 146
Answers will vary. Possible dimensions include: 5 x 18, 6 x 15, 9 x 10

Page 147

	Type of Coin	Number of Coins	Total Amount
Shelly	pennies	29	$.29
Sophie	half-dollars	34	$17.00
Tyler	nickels	19	$.95
Hal	dimes	9	$.90
Perlin	quarters	24	$6.00

Pages 148–149
1. 119 m²
2. 139 ft²
3. 214 in²
4. 166 cm²
5. 171 mi²
6. 235 yd²

Page 150
1. 145 × 23 = 3,335
2. 5,312 ÷ 4 = 1,328
3. 4,531 × 2 = 9,062
4. 1,524 ÷ 3 = 508
5. 1 + 2 + 3 × 4 − 5 = 10
6. 675 × 89 = 60,075
7. 5,976 ÷ 8 = 747

Page 151
1. 13   2. 37
3. 508   4. 285
5. 93   6. 471
7. 7,707   8. 23,215

Page 152
1. 8 fish, 2 snails, 2 plants, 2 rocks
2. 1 fish, 6 snails, 9 plants, 1 rock
3. 5 fish, 1 snail, 2 plants, 4 rocks
4. 6 fish, 3 snails, 5 plants, 4 rocks
5. 3 fish, 9 snails, 7 plants, 3 rocks
6. 10 fish, 3 snails, 1 plant, 1 rock

Page 153
1. 25, 100
2. 46, 97
3. ÷ 2, − 7
4. 470, 490, + 20, − 50
5. 180, 540, 610, + 35
6. 215, 1,075, × 5

Page 154
1. grade 3; math
2. grade 5; reading
3. grade 2; art
4. grade 4; science

Page 155
1. Saturday: 87°F, 65°F
2. Sunday   18
   Monday   20
   Tuesday   18
   Wednesday   15
   Thursday   17
   Friday   16
   Saturday   22
3. 75°F
4. Sunday   77
   Monday   74
   Tuesday   74
   Wednesday   73.5
   Thursday   73.5
   Friday   77
   Saturday   76

Pages 156–157
1. $1,360
2. $829.25
3. $557.94
4. $1,814.70
5. $2,727.27
6. $1,755.38

Page 158
1. 240   2. 4,140
3. 2,970   4. 34,020
5. 165   6. 2,160
7. 1,890   8. 840

Page 159
1. The 2-quart bottle is the best deal at 85 cents per pint. The 1-pint bottle costs 89 cents per pint, and the 1-gallon jug costs 87 cents per pint.
2. The 3-lb bag is the best deal at $1.56 per pound. The 1.5-lb bag is $1.66 per pound, and the 5-lb bag is $1.60 per pound.
3. The 4-ft roll is the best deal at 35 cents per foot. The 2-yd roll is 38 cents per foot, and the 24-in roll is 60 cents per foot.
4. The 12-pack is the best deal at 0.001 cents per sheet. The 8-pack costs 0.0016 cents per sheet and the 10-pack costs 0.0013 cents per sheet.
5. The 1-lb 8-oz box is the best deal at 13 cents per ounce. The 14-oz box is about 21 cents per ounce, and the 10-oz box is about 25 cents per ounce.
6. The 6-pack is the best deal at about 6 cents per ounce. The 8- and 10-pack are both about 7 cents per ounce.

Page 160
1. $\frac{1}{6}$ is colored blue.
   $\frac{1}{6}$ is colored red.
   $\frac{1}{6}$ is colored yellow.
   $\frac{3}{6}$ is colored green.
2. $\frac{3}{9}$ is colored orange.
   $\frac{2}{9}$ is colored purple.
   $\frac{4}{9}$ is colored red.
3. $\frac{5}{10}$ is colored green.
   $\frac{2}{10}$ is colored yellow.
   $\frac{1}{10}$ is colored blue.
   $\frac{2}{10}$ is colored orange.
4. $\frac{2}{5}$ is colored yellow.
   $\frac{1}{5}$ is colored purple.
   $\frac{2}{5}$ is colored blue.

Page 161
1. Magic sum = 34   2. Magic sum = 94

3. Magic sum = 73   4. Magic sum = 81

Page 162
1. $\frac{1}{5}$ is colored green.
   $\frac{1}{5}$ is colored red.
   $\frac{3}{5}$ is colored blue.
2. $\frac{1}{6}$ is colored black.
   $\frac{2}{6}$ is colored yellow.
   $\frac{3}{6}$ is colored red.
3. $\frac{1}{8}$ is colored black.
   $\frac{1}{8}$ is colored white.
   $\frac{2}{8}$ is colored green.
   $\frac{4}{8}$ is colored blue.
4. $\frac{1}{10}$ is colored yellow.
   $\frac{6}{10}$ is colored red.
   $\frac{2}{10}$ is colored orange.
   $\frac{1}{10}$ is colored green.

Page 163
1. $b = 60 ÷ a$; 20, 1
2. $d = c + 11$; 39, 54, 84
3. $f = 35 − e$; 22, 26, 5, 32
4. $h = 7g$; 126, 34, 71, 581

Page 164

Birthday	Amount Received	Total
1	$10	$10
2	$30	$40
3	$50	$90
4	$70	$160
5	$90	$250
6	$110	$360
7	$130	$490
8	$150	$640
9	$170	$810
10	$190	$1,000
11	$210	$1,210
12	$230	$1,440
13	$250	$1,690
14	$270	$1,960
15	$290	$2,250
16	$310	$2,560
17	$330	$2,890
18	$350	$3,240
19	$370	$3,610
20	$390	$4,000

1. 10 years old
2. 20 years old
3. 30 years old
4. 40 years old

Page 165
1. 1 × 24 = 24, 24 × 1 = 24, 2 × 12 = 24, 12 x 2 = 24, 3 × 8 = 24, 8 × 3 = 24, 4 × 6 = 24, 6 × 4 = 24
2. 1 × 48 = 48, 48 × 1 = 48, 2 × 24 = 48, 24 × 2 = 48, 3 × 16 = 48, 16 × 3 = 48, 4 × 12 = 48, 12 × 4 = 48, 6 × 8 = 48, 8 × 6 = 48
3. 1 × 72 = 72, 72 × 1 = 72, 2 × 36 = 72, 36 × 2 = 72, 3 × 24 = 72, 24 × 3 = 72, 4 × 18 = 72, 18 × 4 = 72, 6 × 12 = 72, 12 × 6 = 72, 8 × 9 = 72, 9 × 8 = 72
4. 1 × 120 = 120, 120 × 1 = 120, 2 × 60 = 120, 60 × 2 = 120, 3 × 40 = 120, 40 × 3 = 120, 4 × 30 = 120, 30 × 4 = 120, 5 × 24 = 120, 24 × 5 = 120, 6 × 20 = 120, 20 × 6 = 120, 8 × 15 = 120, 15 × 8 = 120, 10 × 12 = 120, 12 × 10 = 120

Page 166
1. Multiply 6 by 3 to get 18.
2. Yes, 9 + 11 + 13 = 33 and 11 × 3 = 33.
3. Yes, you can just multiply the middle number by 3 to get the sum.

Page 167
1. 40   2. 9
3. 369   4. 78
5. 378   6. 76
7. 153   8. 216

Pages 168–169
1. 3   2. 2
3. 4   4. yes
5. $2.48   6. $19.92

Ingredients	Unit Cost	Number Needed	Total Cost
1 (half-gallon) pineapple soda	$0.89	2	$1.78
1 quart orange sherbet	$1.29	2	$2.58
1 quart vanilla ice cream	$2.99	3	$8.97
1 (32-oz) can tomato sauce	$1.09	2	$2.18
1 bag pizza dough	$1.19	4	$4.76
1 head of broccoli	$0.79	4	$3.16
1 container mushrooms	$2.29	4	$9.16
1 bell pepper	$0.69	8	$5.52
1 onion	$0.52	4	$2.08
1 (6-oz) can black olives	$1.59	4	$6.36
1 package cupcake mix	$2.99	2	$5.98
32-oz Mozzarella Cheese	$4.99	1	$4.99

Page 170

4	3	2	6	8	1	5	9	7
6	8	1	7	5	9	3	2	4
7	5	9	4	3	2	8	1	6
5	1	6	3	9	7	2	4	8
3	9	7	8	2	4	1	6	5
8	2	4	5	1	6	9	7	3
2	7	3	1	4	8	6	5	9
1	4	8	9	6	5	7	3	2
9	6	5	2	7	3	4	8	1

E	H	I	B	D	C	G	A	F
D	C	B	A	F	G	H	I	E
F	G	A	I	E	H	C	B	D
G	B	D	F	H	A	I	E	C
H	A	F	E	C	I	B	D	G
C	I	E	D	G	B	A	F	H
B	E	C	G	A	D	F	H	I
A	D	G	H	I	F	E	C	B
I	F	H	C	B	E	D	G	A

Page 171

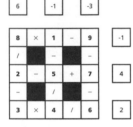

0.9	0.6	0.1	0.7	0.2	0.8	0.5	0.3	0.4
0.2	0.8	0.4	0.5	0.6	0.3	0.7	0.1	0.9
0.7	0.5	0.3	0.9	0.4	0.1	0.6	0.2	0.8
0.1	0.2	0.6	0.4	0.8	0.5	0.3	0.9	0.7
0.4	0.7	0.9	0.1	0.3	0.2	0.8	0.6	0.5
0.5	0.3	0.8	0.6	0.9	0.7	0.2	0.4	0.1
0.8	0.4	0.2	0.3	0.1	0.6	0.9	0.7	0.5
0.6	0.9	0.7	0.2	0.5	0.4	0.1	0.8	0.3
0.3	0.1	0.5	0.8	0.7	0.9	0.4	0.6	0.2

Page 172

Page 173

5	−	4	−	6		-5
−		−		×		
7	+	3	×	1		10
+				−		
8	/	2	−	9		-5

6		-1		-3

8	×	1	−	9		-1
/		−		−		
2	−	5	+	7		4
−				/		
3	×	4	/	6		2

1		-1		-4

Page 174
1. 17,343
2. 34,320
3. 113,040
4. 782,441

Page 175
11 × 1 = 11
12 × 1 = 12
13 × 1 = 13
11 × 11 = 121
12 × 11 = 132
13 × 11 = 143
11 × 111 = 1,221
12 × 111 = 1,332
13 × 111 = 1,443
1. 154
2. 1,665
3. 17,776
4. 188,887
5. 1,999,998
6. 12,221
7. 133,332
8. 1,444,443

Page 176

Players	Hits	At-Bats	Batting Average
Aaron	13	32	.406
Bert	18	27	.667
Charles	9	29	.310
Darnell	11	33	.333
Eli	7	24	.292
Francis	15	31	.484
Gary	19	26	.731
Hassid	23	35	.657
Ian	8	21	.381

Place	Player
1st	Gary
2nd	Bert
3rd	Hassid
4th	Francis
5th	Aaron
6th	Ian
7th	Darnell
8th	Charles
9th	Eli

Page 177
1. <   2. =
3. <   4. >
5. =   6. >
7. =   8. <

Pages 178–179
1.

Each slice stands for 2 people.

2.

Each slice stands for 3 people.

3.

Each slice stands for 5 people.

4.

Each slice stands for 4 people.

Page 180
The missing numbers are 1.75, 6.25, and 15.75. A square's number is determined by adding the numbers to the left, top, and top-left of it.

Page 181
1.
A B C D E F G H I J K
0 .10 .20 .30 .40 .50 .60 .70 .80 .90 1

2.
A B C D E
0 .25 .50 .75 1

3.
A B C
0 0.5 1

4.
A B C D E F
0 0.2 0.4 0.6 0.8 1

Page 182–183
1. Phillip went to the store. He spent $15.42. He gave the cashier $20. What was his change? $4.58
2. Elaine likes to walk. She walked 3.21 miles on Monday, 4.73 miles on Tuesday, and 6.05 miles on Wednesday. How many miles did she walk altogether? 13.99 miles
3. Nathaniel gets up at 8:05 AM for school. It takes him 34 minutes to get ready for school. He leaves when he is ready. What time does Nathaniel leave for school? 8:39 AM
4. At a bake sale, Ellie sold 4 dozen cookies before lunch. After lunch, she sold another 5 dozen cookies. When it was time to leave, she had 1 $\frac{1}{2}$ dozen cookies left. How many cookies did Ellie have at the start of the bake sale? 126 cookies
5. Louis has 2,523 baseball cards. Harold has 4,862 baseball cards. Damian has 3,957 baseball cards. How many baseball cards do Louis, Harold, and Damian have altogether? 11,342 baseball cards

Page 184

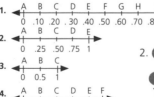

⬡ = 5

♥ = 8

⬠ = 7

▱ = 3

◣ = 9

▽ = 4

○ = 2

Page 185
1. ▲ + ■ = 6

▲	■
6	0
5	1
4	2
2	4
1	5
0	6

2. ⬤ × ■ = 24

⬤	■
1	24
2	12
3	8
4	6
6	4
8	3
12	2
24	1

3. e + q = 10

e	q
0	10
1	9
2	8
3	7
4	6
6	4
7	3
8	2
9	1
10	0

4. h × i = 60

h	i
1	60
2	30
3	20
4	15
5	12
6	10
10	6
12	5
15	4
20	3
30	2
60	1